Knitting Peppa Pig

Over 20 adorable knitted toy patterns for hours of fun!

Cilla Webb

DAVID & CHARLES
— PUBLISHING —

www.davidandcharles.com

Contents

Introduction

Welcome to the wonderful world of Peppa Pig! In this book, you'll meet Peppa Pig, her family, and lots of her playgroup friends. The knitted toy collection in this book will keep the little ones in your life entertained for hours! If you can't decide which one to make first, why not ask them for their favourite?

This book contains all the information needed to create your own set of marvellous Peppa Pig characters. The essential information pages cover the yarn choices, tools and materials needed for your project and the techniques will help you master the different stitches used in the patterns.

Let's jump in!

Tools and Materials

The projects in this book use very easy knitting techniques to create your favourite characters – but they do require a fair bit of sewing up! Here is some information about the yarns and tools required for your projects.

Needles

The patterns in this book have been knitted using 3.5mm (US size 4) straight needles, which is two sizes smaller than that suggested on the yarn band by the manufacturer. This allows for the finished fabric to be taut, and dense enough to prevent the stuffing from migrating through the knitting. George is knitted using smaller 2.5mm (US size 2) straight needles.

Yarn

The yarn used for the patterns in this book is Stylecraft Special DK (light worsted/8ply), which is a premium acrylic with a huge number of bright colours to choose from – ideal for the characters in the world of Peppa Pig. This yarn is soft, durable, anti-pill and, most importantly, washable in the machine. The colours used for each project are listed in the pattern, but feel free to make your own choices using remnants from your stash.

When choosing the yarn, you can opt for a lighter or heavier yarn weight, but keep in mind that this will make your toy smaller or larger than the original pattern.

Other items

Safety toy stuffing: As with the yarn, choose a stuffing that is washable and suitable for soft toys. Polyester stuffing is lightweight and versatile, and also hypoallergenic.

Tweezers: When stuffing smaller pieces, a pair of tweezers can be your best friend!

Tapestry needle: Needle with a wide eye for the yarn used for sewing pieces together and weaving in yarn ends. It also has a blunt tip to avoid splitting the yarn.

Large-eyed sewing needle: For embroidering the details on faces.

Black embroidery thread (floss): For adding some of the smaller details onto the characters.

Scissors: Small sharp scissors for snipping yarn.

Large fork or 3.5–4cm (1½in) pompom maker: To make the pompom tails for Suzy Sheep and Rebecca Rabbit.

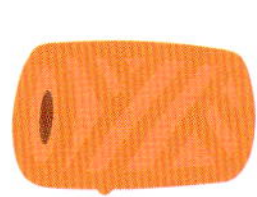

How to Use This Book

All the patterns in this book are worked flat on straight needles and then the pieces are seamed and stuffed, and finally sewn together to make the toy. My preferred method of cast on for toys is the cable cast on method, which creates a smooth, even edge that makes sewing up much easier (see Techniques: Cable Cast On). The toys are mostly knitted in stocking (stockinette) stitch, which is knit stitch on the right side of the work and purl stitch on the wrong side.

Difficulty

Most of the patterns in this book are suitable for beginner knitters with some sewing up skills. Each pattern has a skill level noted at the start of the pattern.

Easy - simple knitting and purling with easy increases and decreases

Intermediate - projects with a lot of sewing, or tricky shaping

Advanced - includes colourwork

Sizing

Peppa and her friends are all the same size so they are perfect for role playing with your favourite characters. The adults are proportionately taller and George and Baby Evie are smaller in comparison.

The measurements in the patterns are from the base of the body to the top of the head, including the ears.

Charts

Two of the patterns have colour charts, either to work a pattern in stranded colourwork or to add it to the finished knitting in duplicate stitch. On each chart, one square is equal to one stitch.

When working stranded colourwork, begin the chart in the bottom right corner, working odd rows from right to left and even rows from left to right. See Techniques: Stranded Colourwork and Techniques: Duplicate Stitch for more information on working these techniques.

Assembling toys

Start by stuffing the body, but don't overstuff because this can make the toys appear lumpy and will alter their shape. Next, position the head on top of the cast-on edge of the body and skewer it into place with two long knitting needles, going through the top of the head to the bottom of the body, at slightly different angles. This will ensure the head stays in position as you sew. Once you're happy with the positioning of the head, start sewing to the body using mattress stitch. When you have nearly closed the gap, insert more stuffing into the neck to give it added sturdiness before closing it up. Insert a knitting needle through the arm, body and other arm to ensure they are level before sewing. Pin the legs into place prior to sewing to ensure they are both facing the right way and are positioned in a straight line.

Abbreviations

g st	garter stitch (every row k)
k	knit
k2tog	knit 2 stitches together (decrease 1 st)
kfb	knit front and back (increase 1 st)
p	purl
p2tog	purl 2 stitches together (decrease 1 st)
psso	pass slipped stitch over (decrease 1 st)
rem	remaining
rep	repeat
RS	right side
sl	slip
ssk	slip 2 stitches knitwise, knit slipped stitches together through back loops (decrease 1 st)
st st	stocking (stockinette) stitch (alt k and p rows)
st(s)	stitch(es)
w&t	wrap and turn (see Techniques: Short Rows)
WS	wrong side
yo	yarn over (see Techniques: Yarn Over Eyelet)
[ ]	work sequence in brackets the number of times stated
*	work sequence from * the number of times stated

Tension (gauge)

Tension is not critical for these projects, but take care not to pull the yarn too tight when working with acrylic yarns. To ensure you achieve the same size toys as specified in the patterns, make a tension swatch using the yarn and needles.

Tension swatch

Cast on 30 sts.

Row 1: K.

Row 2: P.

Rep Rows 1 and 2 thirty times.

Cast (bind) off.

When made in DK (light worsted/8ply) weight acrylic yarn with 3.5mm (US size 4) needles your tension should be 22 sts x 28 rows to 10 x 10cm (4 x 4in). If your tension square is too big, try again with smaller needles. If it is too small, try larger needles.

Safety first!

Anyone dealing with children will know they like to figure out the ins and outs of their toys and usually end up chomping on parts or pulling things apart. Ensure that all parts are securely attached and that your knitted fabric has a tight tension (gauge) so the stuffing can't be removed through any small gaps.

The eyes on all the toys in this book have been embroidered to reduce the risk of little people pulling out the toy safety eyes. However, if the recipient of your toys has surpassed the chewing stage, you could use toy safety eyes instead of embroidering them.

The Projects

Peppa Pig

Peppa is a fun-loving, and sometimes mischievous, little pig. She is four years old and lives with Mummy and Daddy Pig, her little brother George and new baby sister, Evie. Peppa loves to act, sing, dance and make up stories. Most of all, Peppa loves jumping up and down in muddy puddles!

Finished size

28cm (11in)

Needles

3.5mm (US size 4) straight needles

Other tools and materials

- Small amount of black embroidery thread (floss)
- Toy stuffing
- Tapestry needle

Yarn

Samples are made with Stylecraft Special DK (100% acrylic), DK (light worsted) weight, 295m (322yd) per 100g (3½oz) ball in the following shades:

- 35g Candyfloss (1130)
- 10g White (1001)
- 10g Fondant (1241)
- 10g Black (1002)
- 20g Pomegranate (1083)
- Small amounts of Raspberry (1023) and Bright Pink (1435)

Head

Start from back of head. Using Candyfloss, cast on 16 sts.

Row 1: [Kfb, k1] 8 times. (24 sts)

Row 2 and all even rows: P.

Row 3: [K1, kfb, k1] 8 times. (32 sts)

Row 5: [K2, kfb, k1] 8 times. (40 sts)

Row 7: [K3, kfb, k1] 8 times. (48 sts)

Row 9: [K4, kfb, k1] 8 times. (56 sts)

Rows 10–28: Starting with a p row, st st 19 rows.

Row 29: K1, ssk, k to last 3 sts, k2tog, k1. (54 sts)

Row 30: P.

Rows 31–36: Rep Rows 29 and 30. (48 sts)

Row 37: Cast (bind) off 2 sts, k to end. (46 sts)

Row 38: Cast (bind) off 2 sts, p to end. (44 sts)

Row 39: Cast (bind) off 2 sts, k to end. (42 sts)

Row 40: Cast (bind) off 2 sts, p to end. (40 sts)

Rows 41 and 42: K.

Row 43: [K2, k2tog, k1] 8 times. (32 sts)

Row 45: [K1, k2tog, k1] 8 times. (24 sts)

Row 47: [K2tog, k1] 8 times. (16 sts)

Row 49: [K2tog] 8 times. (8 sts)

Break yarn and thread through rem sts. Pull tight and fasten off **(A)**.

Body

Start from neck. Using Candyfloss, cast on 24 sts.

Rows 1 and 2: Starting with a k row, st st 2 rows.

Row 3: [K1, kfb, k1] 8 times. (32 sts)

Row 4 and all even rows: P.

Row 5: [K2, kfb, k1] 8 times. (40 sts)

Row 7: [K3, kfb, k1] 8 times. (48 sts)

Row 9: [K4, kfb, k1] 8 times. (56 sts)

Rows 10–28: Starting with a p row, st st 19 rows.

Row 29: [K4, k2tog, k1] 8 times. (48 sts)

Row 31: [K3, k2tog, k1] 8 times. (40 sts)

Row 33: [K2, k2tog, k1] 8 times. (32 sts)

Row 35: [K1, k2tog, k1] 8 times. (24 sts)

Row 37: [K2tog, k1] 8 times. (16 sts)

Row 39: [K2tog] 8 times. (8 sts)

Break yarn and thread through rem sts. Pull tight and fasten off.

Arms

(make 2)

Using Candyfloss, cast on 5 sts.

Row 1: K.

Row 2: Cast on 2 sts, p to end. (7 sts)

Row 3: Cast on 2 sts, k to end. (9 sts)

Rows 4–24: Starting with a p row, st st 21 rows.

Row 25: K1, [k2tog] 4 times. (5 sts)

Break yarn and thread through rem sts. Pull tight and fasten off.

Fingers

(make 2 per arm)

Using Candyfloss, cast on 5 sts.

Row 1: K.

Row 2: Cast on 2 sts, p to end. (7 sts)

Row 3: Cast on 2 sts, k to end. (9 sts)

Rows 4–6: Starting with a p row, st st 3 rows.

Row 7: K1, [k2tog] 4 times. (5 sts)

Break yarn and thread through rem sts. Pull tight and fasten off.

Ears

(make 2)

Using Candyfloss, cast on 18 sts.

Rows 1–6: Starting with a k row, st st 6 rows.

Row 7: [K2tog, k1] 6 times. (12 sts)

Row 8: P.

Row 9: [K2tog] 6 times. (6 sts)

Break yarn and thread through rem sts. Pull tight and fasten off.

Tail

Using Candyfloss, cast on 25 sts.

Row 1: [Kfb] 25 times. (50 sts)

Cast (bind) off **(B)**.

Eyes

(make 2)

Using White, cast on 14 sts.

Row 1: P.

Row 2: [K2tog] 7 times. (7 sts)

Break yarn and thread through rem sts. Pull tight and fasten off.

Cheeks

(make 2)

Using Fondant, cast on 28 sts.

Row 1: P.

Row 2: [K2tog] 14 times. (14 sts)

Row 3: [P2tog] 7 times. (7 sts)

Break yarn and thread through rem sts. Pull tight and fasten off **(C)**.

Legs

(make 2)

Using Candyfloss, cast on 10 sts.

Rows 1–19: Starting with a k row, st st 19 rows.

Cast (bind) off.

A

B

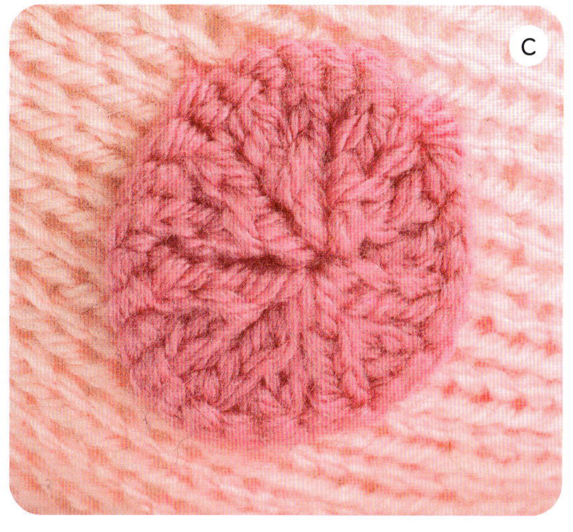

C

Shoes

(make 2)

Using Black, cast on 6 sts.

Row 1: [Kfb] 6 times. (12 sts)

Rows 2–14: Starting with a p row, st st 13 rows.

Row 15: [K2tog] 6 times. (6 sts)

Break yarn and thread through rem sts. Pull tight and fasten off **(D)**.

Dress

Start from bottom of dress. Using Pomegranate, cast on 72 sts.

Rows 1–4: G st 4 rows.

Rows 5–24: Starting with a k row, st st 20 rows.

Row 25: [K6, k2tog, k1] 8 times. (64 sts)

Row 26 and all even rows: P.

LEFT BACK

Work on first 16 sts only.

Row 27: [K5, k2tog, k1] 2 times. (14 sts)

Row 29: [K4, k2tog, k1] 2 times. (12 sts)

Row 31: [K3, k2tog, k1] 2 times. (10 sts)

Row 33: [K2, k2tog, k1] 2 times. (8 sts)

Break yarn.

FRONT

Rejoin yarn to centre 32 sts, work these 32 sts only.

Row 27: [K5, k2tog, k1] 4 times. (28 sts)

Row 29: [K4, k2tog, k1] 4 times. (24 sts)

Row 31: [K3, k2tog, k1] 4 times. (20 sts)

Row 33: [K2, k2tog, k1] 4 times. (16 sts)

Break yarn.

Tip

When assembling the head to the body, skewer a knitting needle through the top of Peppa's head and body to ensure they are positioned correctly.

RIGHT BACK

Rejoin yarn to last 16 sts and rep Rows 27–33 of left back.

Row 34: K8, join and k 16 sts for front, then join and k last 8 sts. (32 sts)

Cast (bind) off knitwise.

Assembly

Sew all seams using mattress stitch (see Techniques: Sewing Up).

Join side seam of head and stuff. Join edges of each cheek to make a circle, then sew cheeks to face using photo as a guide for position. Join edges of each eye to make a circle, then sew each eye above a cheek. Using black embroidery thread (floss) and satin stitch (see Techniques: Satin Stitch), sew a pupil in each eye turned towards snout. Using Fondant, sew an outline around each eye using chain stitch (see Techniques: Chain Stitch). Embroider a curved smile in straight stitch (see Techniques: Straight Stitch) below snout using Bright Pink, then work back to fill gaps between stitches for a solid line. Embroider nostrils in satin stitch at end of snout using Raspberry **(E)**. Fold ears in half, sew along side seam and then secure each ear to top of head on either side.

Join side seam of body and stuff. Sew side seam of dress, leaving small gap for tail, then place dress on body. Position head on cast-on edge of body, with snout slightly tilted upwards, and sew in place.

Sew side seams of arms and each finger. Sew two fingers on either side of end on each arm. Sew side seams of legs and shoes. Stuff shoes lightly, then gather cast-on edge to close. Sew a shoe to bottom of each leg. Using openings in dress as a guide, secure arms and tail to body. Finally, secure both legs to bottom of body.

Weave in all ends (see Techniques: Weaving in Ends).

Tip

Try not to overstuff your toy as the stuffing will show through the stitches.

Peppa's Teddy

Finished size

12cm (4¾in)

Needles

3.5mm (US size 4) straight needles

Other tools and materials

- Toy stuffing
- Small amount of black embroidery thread (floss)
- Tapestry needle

Yarn

Samples are made with Stylecraft Special DK (100% acrylic), DK (light worsted) weight, 295m (322yd) per 100g (3½oz) ball in the following shades:

- 15g Gold (1709)
- 10g White (1001)
- 5g Gingerbread (1806)
- 5g Raspberry (1023)

Head

Start at back of head. Using Gold, cast on 8 sts.

Row 1: [Kfb] 8 times. (16 sts)

Row 2 and all even rows: P.

Row 3: [Kfb, k1] 8 times. (24 sts)

Row 5: [K1, kfb, k1] 8 times. (32 sts)

Rows 6–16: Starting with a p row, st st 11 rows.

Row 17: K1, ssk, k to last 3 sts, k2tog, k1. (30 sts)

Row 18: P.

Rows 19–24: Rep Rows 17 and 18 three times. (24 sts)

Row 25: [K2tog, k1] 8 times. (16 sts)

Rows 26–28: Starting with a p row, st st 3 rows.

Row 29: [K2tog] 8 times. (8 sts)

Break yarn and thread through rem sts. Pull tight and fasten off.

Body

Start at neck. Using Gold, cast on 16 sts.

Rows 1 and 2: Starting with a k row, st st 2 rows.

Row 3: [Kfb, k1] 8 times. (24 sts)

Rows 4–14: Starting with a k row, st st 11 rows.

Row 15: [K2tog, k1] 8 times. (16 sts)

Row 16: P.

Row 17: [K2tog] 8 times. (8 sts)

Break yarn and thread through rem sts. Pull tight and fasten off.

Ears

(make 2)

Using Gold, cast on 10 sts.

Rows 1 and 2: Starting with a k row, st st 2 rows.

Row 3: [K2tog, k1, k2tog] 2 times. (6 sts)

Row 4: P.

Row 5: [P2tog] 6 times. (3 sts)

Break yarn and thread through rem sts. Pull tight and fasten off.

Eyes

(make 2)

Using White, cast on 10 sts.

Row 1: [K2tog] 5 times. (5 sts)

Break yarn and thread through rem sts. Pull tight and fasten off.

Arms

(make 2)

Start from top of arm. Using Gold, cast on 6 sts.

Row 1: K.

Row 2: Cast on 2 sts, p to end. (8 sts)

Row 3: Cast on 2 sts, k to end. (10 sts)

Rows 4–8: Starting with a p row, st st 5 rows.

Row 9: [K2tog] 5 times. (5 sts)

Break yarn and thread through rem sts. Pull tight and fasten off.

Legs

(make 2)

Start from bottom of foot. Using Gold, cast on 10 sts.

Row 1: [Kfb] 10 times. (20 sts)

Rows 2–4: Starting with a p row, st st 3 rows.

Row 5: K3, [k2tog, k1] 5 times, k2. (15 sts)

Row 6: P.

Row 7: K3, [k2tog] 5 times, k2. (10 sts)

Rows 8–14: Starting with a p row, st st 7 rows.

Row 15: [K2tog] 5 times.

Break yarn and thread through rem sts. Pull tight and fasten off.

Assembly

Sew all seams using mattress stitch (see Techniques: Sewing Up).

Join side seam of head and stuff. Join edges of each eye to make a circle, then sew each eye to either side of head, using photo as a guide. Using black embroidery thread (floss) and satin stitch (see Techniques: Satin Stitch), sew a pupil in each eye. Using Gingerbread, sew an outline around each eye using chain stitch (see Techniques: Chain Stitch). Embroider a curved smile in straight stitch (see Techniques: Straight Stitch) below snout using Raspberry, then work back to fill gaps between stitches for a solid line. Embroider a black nose to front of snout. Fold ears in half, sew side seam and attach to either side of head.

Join side seam of body and stuff. Position head on cast-on edge of body and sew in place.

Sew side seams of arms and legs. Add a small amount of stuffing to foot, then fold cast-on edge in half and sew up. Sew arms and legs to body.

Weave in all ends (see Techniques: Weaving in Ends).

Princess Outfit

Finished size

To fit Peppa and friends

Needles

3.5mm (US size 4) straight needles

Other tools and materials

- Toy stuffing
- Tapestry needle
- Straw for wand

Yarn

Samples are made with Stylecraft Special DK (100% acrylic), DK (light worsted) weight, 295m (322yd) per 100g (3½oz) ball in the following shades:

- 20g Pomegranate (1083)
- 15g Citron (1263)
- 10g Turquoise (1068)
- 10g Grass Green (1821)
- 20g White (1001)

Crown

Using Pomegranate, cast on 36 sts.

Rows 1–8: G st 8 rows.

Break Pomegranate, join in Citron.

Rows 9 and 10: Starting with a k row, st st 2 rows.

Row 11: [K4, kfb, k4] 4 times. (40 sts)

Row 12 and all even rows: P.

Row 13: [K5, kfb, k4] 4 times. (44 sts)

Row 15: K1, ssk, k3, k2tog, turn, leaving rem sts unworked.

Row 16: P6 sts only.

Row 17: K1, ssk, k1, k2tog. (4 sts)

Row 19: K1, sl1, k2tog, psso. (2 sts)

Break yarn and thread through rem sts.

*Rejoin yarn to sts set aside.

Row 15: Ssk, k3, k2tog, turn, leaving rem sts unworked.

Row 16: P5 sts only.

Row 17: Ssk, k1, k2tog. (3 sts)

Row 19: Sl1, k2tog, psso. (1 st)

Break yarn and thread through rem st.*

Rep from * to * until there are 8 sts left.

Rejoin yarn to last 8 sts.

Row 15: Ssk, k3, k2tog, k1. (6 sts)

Row 16: P.

Row 17: Ssk, k1, k2tog, k1. (4 sts)

Row 19: Sl1, k2tog, psso, k1. (2 sts)

Break yarn and thread through rem sts **(A)**.

Gems

(make 2 in each colour)

Using Turquoise/Pomegranate/Grass Green, cast on 10 sts.

Row 1: [K2tog] 5 times. (5 sts)

Break yarn and thread through rem sts. Pull tight and fasten off **(A)**.

Wand

Using Pomegranate, cast on 12 sts.

Rows 1–40: Starting with a k row, st st 40 rows.

Row 41: [K2tog] 6 times. (6 sts)

Break yarn and thread through rem sts. Pull tight and fasten off.

Wand star

(make 2, for front and back)

First point: Using Citron, cast on 4 sts.

Row 1: Kfb, k2, kfb. (6 sts)

Row 2 and all even rows: P.

Row 3: Kfb, k4, kfb. (8 sts)

Row 4: P.

Break yarn.

Make three more points.

Put all points on LH needle and work together as follows:

Rows 5 and 6: Starting with a k row, st st 2 rows. (32 sts)

Row 7: [K1, k2tog, k1] 8 times. (24 sts)

Row 9: [K2tog, k1] 8 times. (16 sts)

Row 10: [P2tog] 8 times. (8 sts)

Break yarn and thread through rem sts **(B)**.

A

B

Wand gems

(make 2)

Using Turquoise, cast on 10 sts

Row 1: [K2tog] 5 times. (5 sts)

Break yarn and thread through rem sts. Pull tight and fasten off.

Wings

(make 2)

Using White, cast on 16 sts.

Row 1: [K1, kfb, k4, kfb, k1] 2 times. (20 sts)

Row 2 and all even rows: P.

Row 3: [K1, kfb, k6, kfb, k1] 2 times. (24 sts)

Row 5: [K1, kfb, k8, kfb, k1] 2 times. (28 sts)

Row 7: [K1, kfb, k10, kfb, k1] 2 times. (32 sts)

Row 9: [K1, kfb, k12, kfb, k1] 2 times. (36 sts)

Rows 10–18: Starting with a p row, st st 9 rows.

Row 19: [K1, k2tog, k12, k2tog, k1] 2 times. (32 sts)

Row 21: [K1, k2tog, k10, k2tog, k1] 2 times. (28 sts)

Row 23: [K1, k2tog, k8, k2tog, k1] 2 times. (24 sts)

Row 25: [K1, k2tog, k6, k2tog, k1] 2 times. (20 sts)

Row 27: [K1, k2tog, k4, k2tog, k1] 2 times. (16 sts)

Row 29: [K2tog] 8 times. (8 sts)

Break yarn and thread through rem sts. Pull tight and fasten off.

Wing straps

(make 2)

Using Pomegranate, cast on 40 sts.

Row 1: Cast (bind) off all sts knitwise **(C)**.

Shoes

(make 2)

Start from bottom of foot. Using Pomegranate, cast on 12 sts.

Row 1: [Kfb] to end. (24 sts)

Row 2 and all even rows: P

Row 3: [K1, kfb, k1] 8 times. (32 sts)

Rows 4–8: Starting with a p row, st st 5 rows.

Row 9: K4, [k2tog, k1] 8 times, k4. (24 sts)

Row 11: K4, [k2tog] 8 times, k4. (16 sts)

Cast (bind) off.

Assembly

Sew all seams using mattress stitch (see Techniques: Sewing Up).

Sew side seam of crown. Fold cast-on edge up towards Row 8 to form base. Join side seam of each gem to make a circle. Sew to peaks of crown.

Sew side seam of wand. Cut straw to size and insert into wand, then close cast-on edge. Place two pieces of star on top of each other with WS together and sew along point edges. Sew to star wand, then sew a gem to front and back of star.

Sew side seam of wings. Place both wings on top of each other and sew along cast-on edges to join. Secure strap to top and bottom of wing base. Repeat on other side.

Fold cast-on edge of shoes in half and sew, then sew side seam.

Weave in all ends (see Techniques: Weaving in Ends).

Difficulty

Rainy Day Outfit

Finished size

To fit Peppa and friends

Needles

3.5mm (US size 4) straight needles

Other tools and materials

- Stitch holder
- Toy stuffing
- Small amount of black embroidery thread (floss)
- Tapestry needle

Yarn

Samples are made with Stylecraft Special DK (100% acrylic), DK (light worsted) weight, 295m (322yd) per 100g (3½oz) ball in the following shades:

- 35g Lipstick (1246)
- 20g Fondant (1241)
- 10g Black (1002)

Coat

Start from neck. Using Lipstick, cast on 28 sts.

Rows 1 and 2: G st 2 rows.

Row 3: [K3, kfb, k3] 4 times. (32 sts)

Row 4 and all even rows: K3, p to last 3 sts, k3.

Row 5: [K4, kfb, k1, kfb, k2, kfb, k1, kfb, k4] 2 times. (40 sts)

Row 7: [K5, kfb, k1, kfb, k4, kfb, k1, kfb, k5] 2 times. (48 sts)

Row 9: [K6, kfb, k1, kfb, k6, kfb, k1, kfb, k6] 2 times. (56 sts)

Row 11: [K7, kfb, k1, kfb, k8, kfb, k1, kfb, k7] 2 times. (64 sts)

Row 12: K1, yo, k2tog, p to last 3 sts, k3.

Row 13: [K8, kfb, k1, kfb, k10, kfb, k1, kfb, k8] 2 times. (72 sts)

Row 15: [K9, kfb, k1, kfb, k12, kfb, k1, kfb, k9] 2 times. (80 sts)

Row 17: [K10, kfb, k1, kfb, k14, kfb, k1, kfb, k10] 2 times. (88 sts)

Row 19: [K11, kfb, k1, kfb, k16, kfb, k1, kfb, k11] 2 times. (96 sts)

Row 21: [K12, kfb, k1, kfb, k18, kfb, k1, kfb, k12] 2 times. (104 sts)

Row 22: Break yarn. Slip first 16 sts onto stitch holder, p22 sts for sleeve, leaving rem sts waiting on LH needle (do not work these sts).

FIRST SLEEVE

Work on 22 sts only.

Row 23: Cast on 2 sts, k to end. (24 sts)

Row 24: Cast on 2 sts, p to end. (26 sts)

Rows 25–28: Starting with a k row, st st 4 rows.

Cast (bind) off purlwise.

SECOND SLEEVE

Row 22: Slip next 28 sts on LH needle onto stitch holder, p22 sts for second sleeve, leaving 16 rem sts waiting on LH needle (do not work these sts).

Work as first sleeve.

MAIN BODY

With WS (purl side) facing, place all sts from stitch holders back onto LH needle. (60 sts)

Row 22: K3, p13, turn, cast on 2 sts using cable method, turn, p28, turn, cast on 2 sts using cable method, turn, p to last 3 sts, k3. (64 sts)

Row 23: K.

Row 24: K1, yo, k2tog, p to last 3 sts, k3.

Row 25: K.

Row 26: K3, p to last 3 sts, k3.

Hood chart

Each square represents one stitch. Work odd number rows from right to left and even number rows from left to right.

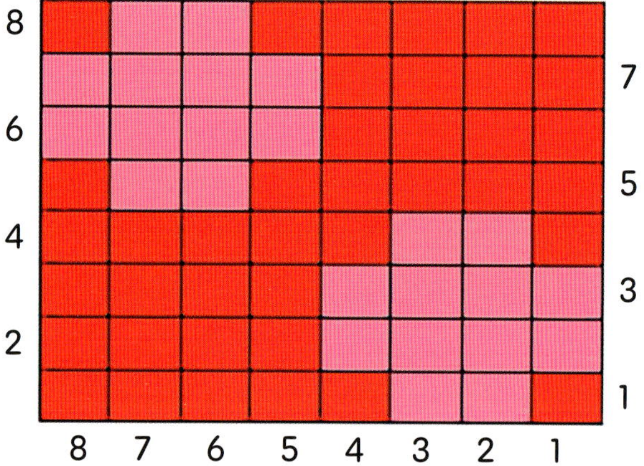

Tip

If you prefer you can make the hood in Lipstick only and add the spots following the chart using duplicate stitch.

Rows 27–34: Rep Rows 25 and 26 four times.

Rows 35 and 36: Rep Rows 23 and 24.

Rows 37–46: Rep Rows 25 and 26 five times.

Rows 47 and 48: K 2 rows.

Cast (bind) off.

Hood

Worked in stranded colourwork (see Techniques: Stranded Colourwork). Using Lipstick, cast on 30 sts.

Row 1: K.

Row 2: K3, p to last 3 sts, k3.

Join in Fondant.

Row 3: K3, rep chart row 1 three times, k3.

Row 4: K3, rep chart row 2 three times, k3.

Row 5: K3, rep chart row 3 three times, k3.

Row 6: K3, rep chart row 4 three times, k3.

Row 7: K3, rep chart row 5 three times, k3.

Row 8: K3, rep chart row 6 three times, k3.

Row 9: K3, rep chart row 7 three times, k3.

Row 10: K3, rep chart row 8 three times, k3.

Rows 11–26: Rep Rows 3–10 twice more.

Cast (bind) off.

Buttons

(make 3)

Using Black, cast on 10 sts.

Row 1: [K2tog] 5 times.

Break yarn and pull through rem sts. Pull tight and fasten off.

Boots

(make 2)

Start from bottom of foot. Using Lipstick, cast on 12 sts.

Row 1: [Kfb] to end. (24 sts)

Row 2: P.

Row 3: [K1, kfb, k1] 8 times. (32 sts)

Row 4: K.

Rows 5–8: Starting with a k row, st st 4 rows.

Row 9: K4, [k2tog, k1] 8 times, k4. (24 sts)

Row 10: P.

Row 11: K4, [k2tog] 8 times, k4. (16 sts)

Rows 12–16: Starting with a p row, st st 5 rows.

Cast (bind) off **(A)**.

Assembly

Sew all seams using mattress stitch (see Techniques: Sewing Up).

Sew side seam of sleeves and close gap between sleeves and main body. Join side seam of buttons to create circle. Sew buttons to front of coat, opposite yarn-overs.

Fold cast- (bound-) off edge of hood in half and sew seam. Sew cast-on edge of hood to cast-on edge of coat.

Using Fondant and duplicate stitch (see Techniques: Duplicate Stitch), sew Hood Chart pattern onto coat, sleeves and hood **(B)**.

Fold cast-on edge of boots in half and sew along seam, then sew up side seam.

Weave in all ends (see Techniques: Weaving in Ends).

George

George is Peppa's two-year-old brother. His favourite thing is his toy dinosaur, which was a gift from Granny and Grandpa Pig. He brings it on all his adventures! George has lots of energy and is very good at climbing. He recently became a big brother and has his own new dinosaur-themed bedroom.

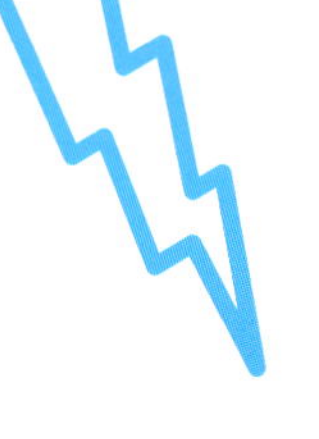

Finished size

22cm (8¾in)

Needles

2.5mm (US size 2) straight needles

Other tools and materials

- Small amount of black embroidery thread (floss)
- Toy stuffing
- Tapestry needle

Yarn

Samples are made with Stylecraft Special DK (100% acrylic), DK (light worsted) weight, 295m (322yd) per 100g (3½oz) ball in the following shades:

- 35g Candyfloss (1130)
- 15g Aster (1003)
- 10g White (1001)
- 10g Fondant (1241)
- 10g Black (1002)
- Small amounts of Raspberry (1023) and Bright Pink (1435)

Head

Start from back of head. Using Candyfloss, cast on 16 sts.

Row 1: [Kfb, k1] 8 times. (24 sts)

Row 2 and all even rows: P.

Row 3: [K1, kfb, k1] 8 times. (32 sts)

Row 5: [K2, kfb, k1] 8 times. (40 sts)

Row 7: [K3, kfb, k1] 8 times. (48 sts)

Row 9: [K4, kfb, k1] 8 times. (56 sts)

Rows 10–28: Starting with a p row, st st 19 rows.

Row 29: K1, ssk, k to last 3 sts, k2tog, k1. (54 sts)

Row 30: P.

Rows 31–36: Rep Rows 29 and 30. (48 sts)

Row 37: Cast (bind) off 2 sts, k to end. (46 sts)

Row 38: Cast (bind) off 2 sts, p to end. (44 sts)

Row 39: Cast (bind) off 2 sts, k to end. (42 sts)

Row 40: Cast (bind) off 2 sts, p to end. (40 sts)

Rows 41 and 42: K.

Row 43: [K2, k2tog, k1] 8 times. (32 sts)

Row 45: [K1, k2tog, k1] 8 times. (24 sts)

Row 47: [K2tog, k1] 8 times. (16 sts)

Row 49: [K2tog] 8 times. (8 sts)

Break yarn and thread through rem sts. Pull tight and fasten off.

Body

Start from neck. Using Aster, cast on 24 sts.

Rows 1 and 2: Starting with a k row, st st 2 rows.

Row 3: [K1, kfb, k1] 8 times. (32 sts)

Row 4 and all even rows: P.

Row 5: [K2, kfb, k1] 8 times. (40 sts)

Row 7: [K3, kfb, k1] 8 times. (48 sts)

Row 9: [K4, kfb, k1] 8 times. (56 sts)

Rows 10–28: Starting with a p row, st st 19 rows.

Row 29: [K4, k2tog, k1] 8 times. (48 sts)

Row 31: [K3, k2tog, k1] 8 times. (40 sts)

Row 33: [K2, k2tog, k1] 8 times. (32 sts)

Row 35: [K1, k2tog, k1] 8 times. (24 sts)

Row 37: [K2tog, k1] 8 times. (16 sts)

Row 39: [K2tog] 8 times. (8 sts)

Break yarn and thread through rem sts. Pull tight and fasten off.

Arms

(make 2)

Using Candyfloss, cast on 5 sts.

Row 1: K.

Row 2: Cast on 2 sts, p to end. (7 sts)

Row 3: Cast on 2 sts, k to end. (9 sts)

Rows 4–24: Starting with a p row, st st 21 rows.

Row 25: K1, [k2tog] 4 times. (5 sts)

Break yarn and thread through rem sts. Pull tight and fasten off.

Fingers

(make 2 per arm)

Using Candyfloss, cast on 5 sts.

Row 1: K.

Row 2: Cast on 2 sts, p to end. (7 sts)

Row 3: Cast on 2 sts, k to end. (9 sts)

Rows 4–6: Starting with a p row, st st 3 rows.

Row 7: K1, [k2tog] 4 times. (5 sts)

Break yarn and thread through rem sts. Pull tight and fasten off.

Ears

(make 2)

Using Candyfloss, cast on 18 sts.

Rows 1–6: Starting with a k row, st st 6 rows.

Row 7: [K2tog, k1] 6 times. (12 sts)

Row 8: P.

Row 9: [K2tog] 6 times. (6 sts)

Break yarn and thread through rem sts. Pull tight and fasten off **(A)**.

Tail

Using Candyfloss cast on 25 sts.

Row 1: [Kfb] 25 times. (50 sts)

Cast (bind) off.

Eyes

(make 2)

Using White, cast on 14 sts.

Row 1: P.

Row 2: [K2tog] 7 times. (7 sts)

Break yarn and thread through rem sts. Pull tight and fasten off.

Cheeks

(make 2)

Using Fondant, cast on 28 sts.

Row 1: P.

Row 2: [K2tog] 14 times. (14 sts)

Row 3: [P2tog] 7 times. (7 sts)

Break yarn and thread through rem sts. Pull tight and fasten off.

Legs

(make 2)

Using Candyfloss, cast on 10 sts.

Rows 1–19: Starting with a k row, st st 19 rows.

Cast (bind) off.

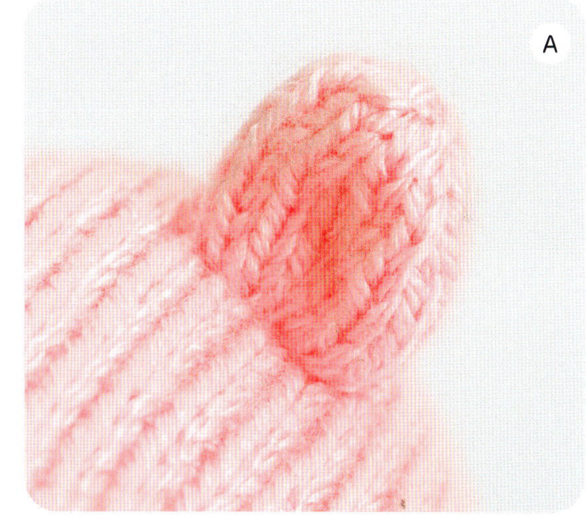

A

B

Shoes

(make 2)

Using Black, cast on 6 sts.

Row 1: [Kfb] 6 times. (12 sts)

Rows 2–14: Starting with a p row, st st 13 rows.

Row 15: [K2tog] 6 times. (6 sts)

Break yarn and thread through rem sts. Pull tight and fasten off **(B)**.

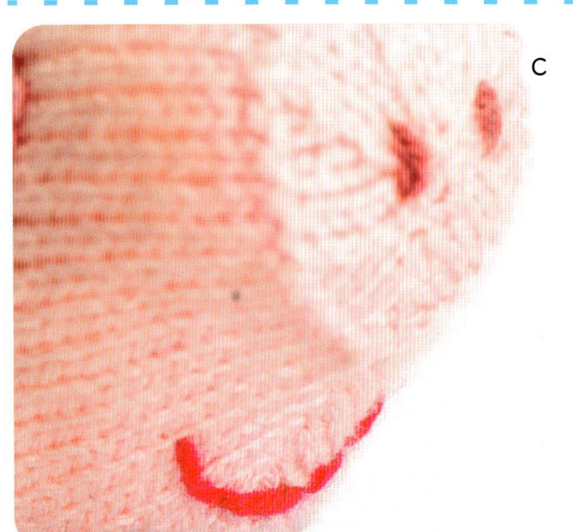

Assembly

Sew all seams using mattress stitch (see Techniques: Sewing Up).

Join side seam of head and stuff. Join edges of each cheek to make a circle, then sew cheeks to face using photo as a guide for position. Join edges of each eye to make a circle, then sew each eye above a cheek. Using black embroidery thread (floss) and satin stitch (see Techniques: Satin Stitch), sew a pupil in each eye turned towards snout. Using Fondant, sew an outline around each eye using chain stitch (see Techniques: Chain Stitch). Embroider a curved smile in straight stitch (see Techniques: Straight Stitch) below snout using Bright Pink, then work back to fill gaps between stitches for a solid line. Embroider nostrils in satin stitch at end of snout using Raspberry **(C)**. Fold ears in half, sew along side seam and then secure each ear to top of head on either side.

Join side seam of body and stuff. Position head on cast-on edge of body, with snout slightly tilted upwards, and sew in place.

Sew side seams of arms and each finger. Sew two fingers on either side of end on each arm **(D)**. Sew an arm on each side of body, using the photo as a guide for position. Sew side seams of legs and shoes. Stuff shoes lightly, then gather cast-on edge to close. Sew a shoe to bottom of each leg, then sew each leg to bottom of body.

Sew tail to centre back at bottom of body.

Weave in all ends (see Techniques: Weaving in Ends).

Tip

Embroidering facial features can take some practice. Don't hesitate to undo them and try again if you're not 100% satisfied with the result.

Difficulty

George's Dinosaur

Finished size

21cm (8¼in) tall sitting, to top spike

Needles

3.5mm (US size 4) straight needles

Other tools and materials

- Toy stuffing
- Small amount of black embroidery thread (floss)
- Tapestry needle

Yarn

Samples are made with Stylecraft Special DK (100% acrylic), DK (light worsted) weight, 295m (322yd) per 100g (3½oz) ball in the following shades:

- 20g Kelly Green (1826)
- 15g Bottle (1009)
- 10g Lipstick (1246)
- 5g White (1001)
- 15g Sage (1725)

Head

Start from neck. Using Kelly Green, cast on 24 sts.

Row 1 (WS) and all odd rows: P.

Row 2: [Kfb, k1] 12 times. (36 sts)

Rows 3–5: Starting with a p row, st st 3 rows.

Row 6: K24, w&t, p12, w&t, k10, w&t, p8, w&t, k to end.

Row 8: Cast (bind) off 12 sts, k11 (12 sts on right-hand needle), cast (bind) off 12 sts. (12 sts)

Rejoin yarn to 12 sts.

Row 9:  Cast on 12 sts using cable cast on, p to end. (24 sts)

Row 10: Cast on 12 sts using cable cast on, k to end. (36 sts)

Row 12: K24, w&t, p12, w&t, k10, w&t, p8, w&t, k to end.

Rows 13–15: Starting with a p row, st st 3 rows.

Row 16: [K2tog] 18 times. (18 sts)

Cast (bind) off.

Body

Using Kelly Green, cast on 24 sts.

Rows 1–14: Starting with a k row, st st 14 rows.

Row 15: [K1, kfb, k1] 8 times. (32 sts)

Row 16 and all even rows: P.

Row 17: K24, w&t, p16, w&t, k14, w&t, p12, w&t, k10, w&t, p8, w&t, k to end.

Rows 18–22: Starting with a p row, st st 5 rows.

Row 23: K24, w&t, p16, w&t, k14, w&t, p12, w&t, k10, w&t, p8, w&t, k to end.

Rows 24–26: Starting with a p row, st st 3 rows.

Row 27: [K5, k2tog, k1] 4 times. (28 sts)

Rows 28–30: Starting with a p row, st st 3 rows.

Row 31: [K4, k2tog, k1] 4 times. (24 sts)

Rows 32–34: Starting with a p row, st st 3 rows.

Row 35: [K3, k2tog, k1] 4 times. (20 sts)

Rows 36–38: Starting with a p row, st st 3 rows.

Row 39: [K2, k2tog, k1] 4 times. (16 sts)

Rows 40–42: Starting with a p row, st st 3 rows.

Row 43: [K1, k2tog, k1] 4 times. (12 sts)

Rows 44–46: Starting with a p row, st st 3 rows.

Row 47: [K2tog, k1] 4 times. (8 sts)

Rows 48–50: Starting with a p row, st st 3 rows.

Row 51: [K2tog] 4 times. (4 sts)

Break yarn and thread through rem sts. Pull tight and fasten off.

Mouth

Using Lipstick, cast on 4 sts.

Row 1: Kfb, k2, kfb. (6 sts)

Rows 2–4: Starting with a p row, st st 3 rows.

Row 5: Kfb, k4, kfb. (8 sts)

Rows 6–8: Starting with a p row, st st 3 rows.

Row 9: Kfb, k6, kfb. (10 sts)

Rows 10–12: Starting with a p row, st st 3 rows.

Row 13: Kfb, k8, kfb. (12 sts)

Rows 14–16: Starting with a p row, st st 3 rows.

Row 17: K2tog, k8, k2tog. (10 sts)

Rows 18–20: Starting with a p row, st st 3 rows.

Row 21: K2tog, k6, k2tog. (8 sts)

Rows 22–24: Starting with a p row, st st 3 rows.

Row 25: K2tog, k4, k2tog. (6 sts)

Rows 26–28: Starting with a p row, st st 3 rows.

Row 29: K2tog, k2, k2tog. (4 sts)

Cast (bind) off.

Teeth

(make 2)

Using White, cast on 5 sts, k2, sl first st over second st, k1, sl first st over second st, sl rem st from right needle to left. (3 sts)

Rep until you have 30 sts.

Cast (bind) off using Bottle **(A)**.

Eyes

(make 2)

Using White, cast on 10 sts

Row 1: [K2tog] 5 times. (5 sts)

Break yarn and thread through rem sts. Pull tight and fasten off **(A)**.

Arms/legs

(make 4)

Using Bottle, cast on 5 sts.

Row 1: K.

Row 2: Cast on 2 sts, p to end. (7 sts)

Row 3: Cast on 2 sts, k to end. (9 sts)

Rows 4–14: Starting with a p row, st st 11 rows.

Row 15: K1, [k2tog] 4 times. (5 sts)

Break yarn and thread through rem sts. Pull tight and fasten off.

Fingers/toes

(make 2 per limb)

Using Bottle, cast on 5 sts.

Row 1: K.

Row 2: Cast on 2 sts, p to end. (7 sts)

Row 3: Cast on 2 sts, k to end. (9 sts)

Rows 4–6: Starting with a p row, st st 3 rows.

Row 7: K1, [k2tog] 4 times. (5 sts)

Break yarn and thread through rem sts. Pull tight and fasten off.

Spikes

(make 8)

Using Sage, cast on 8 sts.

Rows 1 and 2: Starting with a k row, st st 2 rows.

Row 3: [K2tog] 4 times. (4 sts)

Row 4: P.

Row 5: [K2tog] 2 times. (2 sts)

Break yarn and thread through rem sts. Pull tight and fasten off **(B)**.

Assembly

Sew all seams using mattress stitch (see Techniques: Sewing Up).

Join side seam of head. Close cast-on and cast- (bound) off edge and stuff. Secure mouth to front opening of head. Sew row of teeth to top and bottom of mouth **(A)**. Join edges of each eye to make a circle, then sew eyes to either side of head. Using black embroidery thread (floss) and satin stitch (see Techniques: Satin Stitch), sew a pupil in each eye. Using Bottle, sew an outline around each eye in chain stitch (see Techniques: Chain Stitch) **(A)**.

Join side seam of body and stuff. Position head on cast-on edge of body and sew in place.

Sew side seams of arms/legs. Sew side seam of fingers and sew two fingers to each arm/leg. Sew arms and legs to body. Fold spikes in half, sew side seam and attach to back of head and along back of body **(B)**.

Weave in all ends (see Techniques: Weaving in Ends).

Difficulty

Baby Evie

Evie is an incredibly happy baby. Nothing makes her giggle and bounce around more than kissing her heart-shaped birthmark. She loves the sounds of singing, music, and laughing and does her special piggle-wiggle dance when she hears something she likes. Her favourite toy is her rubber duck, affectionately named 'Wakwak' which was gifted to her by her big siblings, Peppa and George.

Finished size

11cm (4¼in)

Needles

3.5mm (US size 4) straight needles

Other tools and materials

- Toy stuffing
- Small amount of black embroidery thread (floss)
- Tapestry needle

Yarn

Samples are made with Stylecraft Special DK (100% acrylic), DK (light worsted) weight, 295m (322yd) per 100g (3½oz) ball in the following shades:

- 15g Candyfloss (1130)
- 15g Spearmint (1842)
- 5g White (1001)
- 5g Fondant (1241)
- 5g Parma Violet (1724)
- 5g Bright Pink (1435)
- 5g Raspberry (1023)
- 5g Citron (1263)

Head

Start from back of head. Using Candyfloss, cast on 8 sts.

Row 1: [Kfb] 8 times. (16 sts)

Row 2 and all even rows: P.

Row 3: [Kfb, k1] 8 times. (24 sts)

Row 5: [K1, kfb, k1] 8 times. (32 sts)

Rows 6–16: Starting with a p row, st st 11 rows.

Row 17: K1, ssk, k to last 3 sts, k2tog, k1. (30 sts)

Row 18: P.

Rows 19–22: Rep Rows 17 and 18. (26 sts)

Row 23: Cast (bind) off 2 sts, k to end. (24 sts)

Row 24: Cast (bind) off 2 sts, p to end. (22 sts)

Row 25: Cast (bind) off 2 sts, k to end. (20 sts)

Row 26: Cast (bind) off 2 sts, p to end. (18 sts)

Rows 27 and 28: K.

Row 29: [K2tog, k1] 6 times. (12 sts)

Row 31: [K2tog] 6 times. (6 sts)

Break yarn and thread through rem sts. Pull tight and fasten off.

Body

Start from neck. Using Spearmint, cast on 16 sts.

Rows 1 and 2: Starting with a k row, st st 2 rows.

Row 3: [Kfb, k1] 8 times. (24 sts)

Row 4 and all even rows: P.

Row 5: [K1, kfb, k1] 8 times. (32 sts)

Rows 6–16: Starting with a p row, st st 11 rows.

Row 17: [K1, k2tog, k1] 8 times. (24 sts)

Row 19: [K2tog, k1] 8 times. (16 sts)

Row 21: [K2tog] 8 times. (8 sts)

Break yarn and thread through rem sts. Pull tight and fasten off.

Arms

(make 2)

Using Spearmint, cast on 5 sts.

Row 1: K.

Row 2: Cast on 2 sts, p to end. (7 sts)

Row 3: Cast on 2 sts, k to end. (9 sts)

Rows 4–8: Starting with a p row, st st 5 rows.

Row 9: K1, [k2tog] 4 times. (5 sts)

Break yarn and thread through rem sts. Pull tight and fasten off.

Ears

(make 2)

Using Candyfloss, cast on 10 sts.

Rows 1–4: Starting with a k row, st st 4 rows.

Row 5: [K2tog, k1, k2tog] 2 times. (6 sts)

Row 6: [P2tog] 3 times. (3 sts)

Break yarn and thread through rem sts. Pull tight and fasten.

Tail

Using Candyfloss, cast on 16 sts.

Row 1: [Kfb] 16 times. (32 sts)

Cast (bind) off **(A)**.

Eyes

(make 2)

Using White cast on 10 sts.

Row 1: [K2tog] 5 times. (5 sts)

Break yarn and thread through rem sts. Pull tight and fasten off.

Cheek

(make 1)

Using Fondant cast on 10 sts.

Row 1: [K2tog] 5 times. (5 sts)

Break yarn and thread through rem. sts. Pull tight and fasten off.

Legs

(make 2)

Using Spearmint, cast on 9 sts.

Rows 1–8: Starting with a k row, st st 8 rows.

Row 9: K1, [k2tog] 4 times. (5 sts)

Break yarn and thread through rem sts. Pull tight and fasten off **(B)**.

Feet

(make two)

Using Spearmint, cast on 5 sts.

Row 1: K1, [kfb] 4 times. (9 sts)

Rows 2–6: Starting with a p row, st st 5 rows.

Row 7: K1, [k2tog] 4 times. (5 sts)

Break yarn and thread through rem sts. Pull tight and fasten off **(B)**.

A

B

Tip

If you're substituting the yarn for a different weight, you will also have to change the needle size to get a similar result. Try needles two sizes smaller than stated on the ball band – but do a tension (gauge) swatch to check the result.

Bow

Using White cast on 16 sts.

Rows 1 and 2: Starting with a k row, st st 2 rows.

Cast (bind) off.

Bib

Using Parma Violet, cast on 10 sts.

Row 1: Kfb, k to last st, kfb. (12 sts)

Rows 2–4: Starting with a p row, st st 3 rows.

Row 5: Ssk, k8, k2tog. (10 sts)

Row 6: P.

Row 7: Ssk, k6, k2tog. (8 sts)

Row 8: P.

Cast (bind) off **(C)**.

Assembly

Sew all seams using mattress stitch (see Techniques: Sewing Up).

Join side seam of head and stuff. Join edges of each eye to make a circle, then sew each eye to head, using photo as a guide for position. Using black embroidery thread (floss) and satin stitch (see Techniques: Satin Stitch), sew a pupil in each eye. Using Fondant, sew an outline around each eye using chain stitch (see Techniques: Chain Stitch). Embroider a curved smile in straight stitch (see Techniques: Straight Stitch) below snout using Bright Pink, then work back to fill gaps between stitches for a solid line. Embroider two nostrils to front of snout in Raspberry. Join edges of cheek to make a circle, then sew cheek to left side of face using photo as a guide for position. Embroider a heart-shape cheek in Fondant on right side of face **(D)**. Fold ears in half, sew side seam and attach to either side at top of head.

Join side seam of body and stuff. Position head on cast-on edge of body and sew in place.

Sew side seams of arms and legs. Add a small amount of stuffing to foot, then fold cast-on edge in half and sew up. Sew foot to cast-on edge of leg. Sew arms and legs to body. Secure tail to back of body.

Join side seam of bow and wrap a length of yarn around middle to cinch it, creating a bow shape. Sew to right ear.

Using Citron, embroider a duck shape on bib using satin stitch **(C)**. Sew bib around neck.

Weave in all ends (see Techniques: Weaving in Ends).

Difficulty

Evie's Rubber Duck

Finished size

7cm (2¾in)

Needles

3.5mm (US size 4) straight needles

Other tools and materials

- Toy stuffing
- Small amount of black embroidery thread (floss)
- Tapestry needle

Yarn

Samples are made with Stylecraft Special DK (100% acrylic), DK (light worsted) weight, 295m (322yd) per 100g (3½oz) ball in the following shades:

- 20g Citron (1263)
- 10g Spice (1711)

Head

Using Citron, cast on 16 sts.

Row 1: [Kfb, k1] 8 times. (24 sts)

Row 2 and all even rows: P.

Row 3: [K1, kfb, k1] 8 times. (32 sts)

Rows 4–10: Starting with a p row, st st 7 rows.

Row 11: [K1, k2tog, k1] 8 times. (24 sts)

Row 13: [K2tog, k1] 8 times. (16 sts)

Row 14: [P2tog] 8 times. (8 sts)

Break yarn and thread through rem sts. Pull tight and fasten off.

Body

Using Citron, cast on 4 sts.

Row 1: [Kfb] 4 times. (8 sts)

Row 2 and all even rows: P.

Row 3: [Kfb, k2, kfb] 2 times. (12 sts)

Row 5: [Kfb, k4, kfb] 2 times. (16 sts)

Row 7: [Kfb, k6, kfb] 2 times. (20 sts)

Row 9: [Kfb, k8, kfb] 2 times. (24 sts)

Row 11: [Kfb, k10, kfb] 2 times. (28 sts)

Row 13: [Kfb, k12, kfb] 2 times. (32 sts)

Rows 14–20: Starting with a p row, st st 7 rows.

Row 21: [K1, k2tog, k1] 8 times. (24 sts)

Row 23: [K2tog, k1] 8 times. (16 sts)

Row 24: [P2tog] 8 times. (8 sts)

Break yarn and thread through rem sts. Pull tight and fasten off.

Beak

(make 2)

Using Spice, cast on 10 sts.

Rows 1–4: Starting with a k row, st st 4 rows.

Row 5: [K2tog] 5 times. (5 sts)

Break yarn and thread through rem sts. Pull tight and fasten off **(A)**.

Assembly

Sew all seams using mattress stitch (see Techniques: Sewing Up).

Sew side seam of head and body and stuff. Secure cast-on edge of head over thicker part of body. Using Black embroidery thread (floss), embroider two eyes either side in satin stitch (see Techniques: Satin Stitch) **(B)**.

Sew side seam of beak. Secure both parts to front of head, one on top of other **(A)**.

Weave in all ends (see Techniques: Weaving in Ends).

A

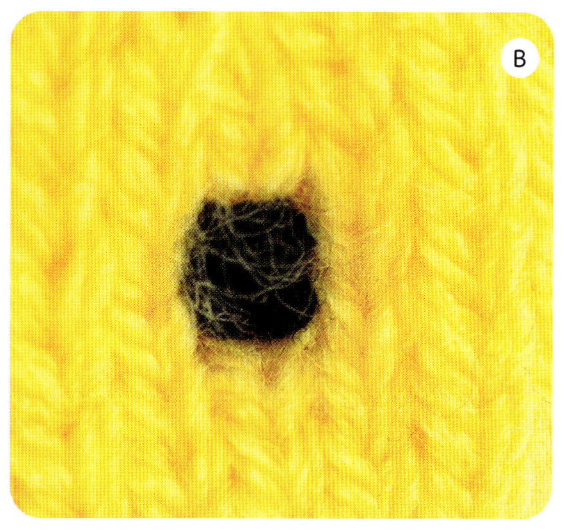
B

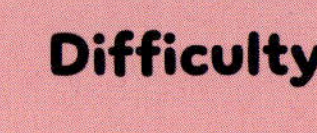

Mummy Pig

Mummy Pig is strong, kind and caring, always offering support and encouragement to her kids. She is so proud of her family and everything they do together. Mummy Pig is also very creative, enjoys cooking, and spends lots of time at her computer writing stories. She loves to spread joy and connect with people wherever she goes. She even volunteers in the Mummies Fire Brigade.

Finished size

34cm (13¼in)

Needles

3.5mm (US size 4) straight needles

Other tools and materials

- Toy stuffing
- Small amount of black embroidery thread (floss)
- Tapestry needle

Yarn

Samples are made with Stylecraft Special DK (100% acrylic), DK (light worsted) weight, 295m (322yd) per 100g (3½oz) ball in the following shades:

- 50g Candyfloss (1130)
- 5g White (1001)
- 10g Fondant (1241)
- 10g Black (1002)
- 30g Clementine (1853)
- 5g Wisteria (1432)
- 5g Bright Pink (1435)
- 5g Raspberry (1023)

Head

Start from back of head. Using Candyfloss, cast on 16 sts.

Row 1: [Kfb, k1] 8 times. (24 sts)

Row 2 and all even rows: P.

Row 3: [K1, kfb, k1] 8 times. (32 sts)

Row 5: [K2, kfb, k1] 8 times. (40 sts)

Row 7: [K3, kfb, k1] 8 times. (48 sts)

Row 9: [K4, kfb, k1] 8 times. (56 sts)

Row 11: [K5, kfb, k1] 8 times. (64 sts)

Rows 12–36: Starting with a p row, st st 25 rows.

Row 37: K1, ssk, k to last 3 sts, k2tog, k1. (62 sts)

Row 38: P.

Rows 39–52: Rep Rows 37 and 38. (48 sts)

Row 53: Cast (bind) off 2 sts, k to end. (46 sts)

Row 54: Cast (bind) off 2 sts, p to end. (44 sts)

Row 55: Cast (bind) off 2, sts, k to end. (42 sts)

Row 56: Cast (bind) off 2 sts, p to end. (40 sts)

Rows 57 and 58: K 2 rows.

Row 59: [K2, k2tog, k1] 8 times. (32 sts)

Row 61: [K1, k2tog, k1] 8 times. (24 sts)

Row 63: [K2tog, k1] 8 times. (16 sts)

Row 65: [K2tog] 8 times. (8 sts)

Break yarn and thread through rem sts. Pull tight and fasten off **(A)**.

Body

Start from neck. Using Candyfloss, cast on 32 sts.

Row 1: [K2, kfb, k1] 8 times. (40 sts)

Row 2 and all even rows: P.

Row 3: [K3, kfb, k1] 8 times. (48 sts)

Row 5: [K4, kfb, k1] 8 times. (56 sts)

Row 7: [K5, kfb, k1] 8 times. (64 sts)

Rows 8–32: Starting with a p row, st st 25 rows.

Row 33: [K5, k2tog, k1] 8 times. (56 sts)

Row 35: [K4, k2tog, k1] 8 times. (48 sts)

Row 37: [K3, k2tog, k1] 8 times. (40 sts)

Row 39: [K2, k2tog, k1] 8 times. (32 sts)

Row 41: [K1, k2tog, k1] 8 times. (24 sts)

Row 43: [K2tog, k1] 8 times. (16 sts)

Row 45: [K2tog] 8 times. (8 sts)

Break yarn and thread through rem sts. Pull tight and fasten off.

Arms

(make two)

Using Candyfloss, cast on 5 sts.

Row 1: K.

Row 2: Cast on 2 sts, p to end. (7 sts)

Row 3: Cast on 2 sts, k to end. (9 sts)

Rows 4–28: Starting with a p row, st st 25 rows.

Row 29: K1, [k2tog] 4 times. (5 sts)

Break yarn and thread through rem sts. Pull tight and fasten off.

Fingers

(make 2 per arm)

Using Candyfloss, cast on 5 sts.

Row 1: K.

Row 2: Cast on 2 sts, p to end. (7 sts)

Row 3: Cast on 2 sts, k to end. (9 sts)

Rows 4–6: Starting with a p row, st st 3 rows.

Row 7: K1, [k2tog] 4 times. (5 sts)

Break yarn and thread through rem sts. Pull tight and fasten off.

Ears

(make 2)

Using Candyfloss, cast on 20 sts.

Rows 1–10: Starting with a k row, st st 10 rows.

Row 11: [K2tog] 10 times. (10 sts)

Row 12: [P2tog] 5 times. (5 sts)

Break yarn and thread through rem sts. Pull tight and fasten off.

Tail

Using Candyfloss, cast on 25 sts.

Row 1: [Kfb] 25 times. (50 sts)

Cast (bind) off.

Eyes

(make 2)

Using White, cast on 20 sts.

Row 1: P.

Row 2: [K2tog] 10 times. (10 sts)

Row 3: [P2tog] 5 times. (5 sts)

Break yarn and thread through rem sts. Pull tight and fasten off **(A)**.

Cheeks

(make 2)

Using Fondant, cast on 32 sts.

Row 1: P.

Row 2: [K2tog] 16 times. (16 sts)

Row 3: P.

Row 4: [K2tog] 8 times. (8 sts)

Break yarn and thread through rem sts. Pull tight and fasten off **(B)**.

Legs

(make 2)

Using Candyfloss, cast on 10 sts.

Rows 1–24: St st 24 rows.

Cast (bind) off.

A

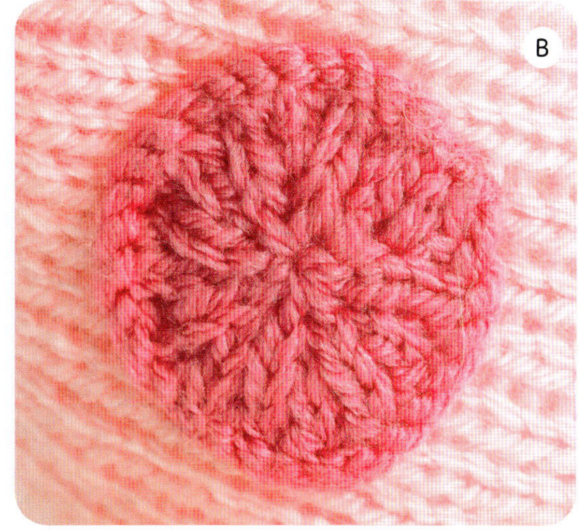

B

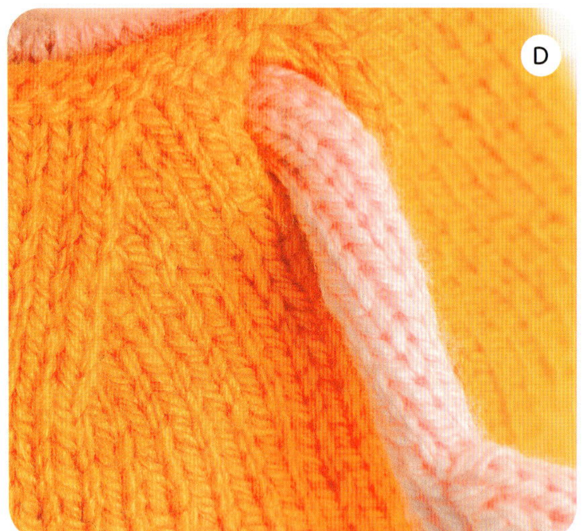

Shoes

(make 2)

Using Black, cast on 8 sts.

Row 1: [Kfb] 8 times. (16 sts)

Rows 2–16: Starting with a p row, st st 14 rows.

Row 17: [K2tog] 8 times. (8 sts)

Break yarn and thread through rem sts. Pull tight and fasten off **(C)**.

Dress

Starting from bottom of dress.

Using Clementine, cast on 80 sts.

Rows 1–4: G st 4 rows.

Rows 5–34: Starting with a k row, st st 30 rows.

Row 35: [K7, k2tog, k1] 8 times. (72 sts)

Row 36 and all even rows: P.

LEFT BACK

Work on first 18 sts only.

Row 37: [K6, k2tog, k1] 2 times. (16 sts)

Row 39: [K5, k2tog, k1] 2 times. (14 sts)

Row 41: [K4, k2tog, k1] 2 times. (12 sts)

Row 43: [K3, k2tog, k1] 2 times. (10 sts)

Break yarn.

FRONT

Rejoin yarn to centre sts, work next 36 sts only.

Row 37: [K6, k2tog, k1] 4 times. (32 sts)

Row 39: [K5, k2tog, k1] 4 times. (28 sts)

Row 41: [K4, k2tog, k1] 4 times. (24 sts)

Row 43: [K3, k2tog, k1] 4 times. (20 sts)

Break yarn.

RIGHT BACK

Rejoin yarn to last 18 sts, rep Rows 37–43 of left back.

Row 44: K10, join and k 20 sts for front, join and k last 10 sts. (40 sts)

Cast (bind) off knitwise **(D)**.

Assembly

Sew all seams using mattress stitch (see Techniques: Sewing Up).

Join side seam of head and stuff. Join edges of each cheek to make a circle, then sew cheeks to face using photo as a guide for position. Join edges of each eye to make a circle, then sew each eye above a cheek. Using black embroidery thread (floss) and satin stitch (see Techniques: Satin Stitch), sew a pupil in each eye turned towards snout. Using Wisteria, sew an outline around each eye using chain stitch (see Techniques: Chain Stitch) and add eyelashes using Black **(E)**. Embroider a curved smile in straight stitch (see Techniques: Straight Stitch) below snout using Bright Pink, then work back to fill gaps between stitches for a solid line. Embroider nostrils in satin stitch using Raspberry. Fold ears in half, sew side seam and then secure each ear to top of head on either side.

Join side seam of body and stuff. Position head on cast-on edge of body and sew in place. Place dress on body then sew side seam, leaving small gap for tail.

Sew side seams of arms and each finger. Sew two fingers on either side of end on each arm. Sew side seams of legs and shoes. Stuff shoes lightly, then gather cast-on edge to close. Secure a shoe to bottom of each leg. Sew legs to bottom of body. Using openings in dress as a guide, sew arms **(D)** and tail to body.

Weave in all ends (see Techniques: Weaving in Ends).

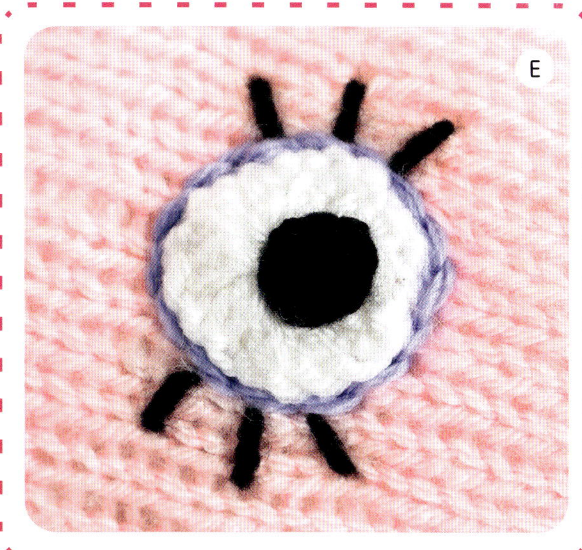

Difficulty

Daddy Pig

Daddy Pig is great at playing and loves having fun with his kids. He is always encouraging them to try new things and inspiring their confidence. He is keen to keep fit and is always looking for new ways to get active. Daddy Pig also enjoys trying new hobbies like magic, drumming and cooking. Daddy Pig's best friend is Mummy Pig and together they make brilliant parents.

Finished size

32cm (12½in)

Needles

3.5mm (US size 4) straight needles

Other tools and materials

- Toy stuffing
- Small amount of black embroidery thread (floss)
- Tapestry needle

Yarn

Samples are made with Stylecraft Special DK (100% acrylic), DK (light worsted) weight, 295m (322yd) per 100g (3½oz) ball in the following shades:

- 40g Candyfloss (1130)
- 15g Spearmint (1842)
- 5g White (1001)
- 10g Fondant (1241)
- 15g Black (1002)
- 5g Raspberry (1023)
- 5g Gingerbread (1806)

Head

Start from back of head. Using Candyfloss, cast on 16 sts.

Row 1: [Kfb, k1] 8 times. (24 sts)

Row 2 and all even rows: P.

Row 3: [K1, kfb, k1] 8 times. (32 sts)

Row 5: [K2, kfb, k1] 8 times. (40 sts)

Row 7: [K3, kfb, k1] 8 times. (48 sts)

Row 9: [K4, kfb, k1] 8 times. (56 sts)

Row 11: [K5, kfb, k1] 8 times. (64 sts)

Rows 12–36: Starting with a p row, st st 25 rows.

Row 37: K1, ssk, k to last 3 sts, k2tog, k1. (62 sts)

Row 38: P.

Rows 39–52: Rep Rows 37 and 38. (48 sts)

Row 53: Cast (bind) off 2 sts, k to end. (46 sts)

Row 54: Cast (bind) off 2 sts, p to end. (44 sts)

Row 55: Cast (bind) off 2, sts, k to end. (42 sts)

Row 56: Cast (bind) off 2 sts, p to end. (40 sts)

Rows 57 and 58: K.

Row 59: [K2, k2tog, k1] 8 times. (32 sts)

Row 61: [K1, k2tog, k1] 8 times. (24 sts)

Row 63: [K2tog, k1] 8 times. (16 sts)

Row 65: [K2tog] 8 times. (8 sts)

Break yarn and thread through rem sts. Pull tight and fasten off.

Body

Start from neck. Using Spearmint, cast on 32 sts.

Row 1: [K2, kfb, k1] 8 times. (40 sts)

Row 2 and all even rows: P.

Row 3: [K3, kfb, k1] 8 times. (48 sts)

Row 5: [K4, kfb, k1] 8 times. (56 sts)

Row 7: [K5, kfb, k1] 8 times. (64 sts)

Rows 8–32: Starting with a p row, st st 25 rows.

Row 33: [K5, k2tog, k1] 8 times. (56 sts)

Row 35: [K4, k2tog, k1] 8 times. (48 sts)

Row 37: [K3, k2tog, k1] 8 times. (40 sts)

Row 39: [K2, k2tog, k1] 8 times. (32 sts)

Row 41: [K1, k2tog, k1] 8 times. (24 sts)

Row 43: [K2tog, k1] 8 times. (16 sts)

Row 45: [K2tog] 8 times. (8 sts)

Break yarn and thread through rem sts. Pull tight and fasten off.

Arms

(make two)

Using Candyfloss, cast on 5 sts.

Row 1: K.

Row 2: Cast on 2 sts, p to end. (7 sts)

Row 3: Cast on 2 sts, k to end. (9 sts)

Rows 4–28: Starting with a p row, st st 25 rows.

Row 29: K1, [k2tog] 4 times. (5 sts)

Break yarn and thread through rem sts. Pull tight and fasten off **(A)**.

Fingers

(make 2 per arm)

Using Candyfloss, cast on 5 sts.

Row 1: K.

Row 2: Cast on 2 sts, p to end. (7 sts)

Row 3: Cast on 2 sts, k to end. (9 sts)

Rows 4–6: Starting with a p row, st st 3 rows.

Row 7: K1, [k2tog] 4 times. (5 sts)

Break yarn and thread through rem sts. Pull tight and fasten off **(A)**.

Ears

(make 2)

Using Candyfloss, cast on 20 sts.

Rows 1–10: Starting with a k row, st st 10 rows.

Row 11: [K2tog] 10 times. (10 sts)

Row 12: [P2tog] 5 times. (5 sts)

Break yarn and thread through rem sts. Pull tight and fasten off.

Tail

Using Candyfloss, cast on 25 sts.

Row 1: [Kfb] 25 times. (50 sts)

Cast (bind) off **(B)**.

Eyes

(make 2)

Using White, cast on 20 sts.

Row 1: P.

Row 2: [K2tog] 10 times. (10 sts)

Row 3: [P2tog] 5 times. (5 sts)

Break yarn and thread through rem sts. Pull tight and fasten off.

Cheeks

(make 2)

Using Fondant, cast on 32 sts.

Row 1: P.

Row 2: [K2tog] 16 times. (16 sts)

Row 3: P.

Row 4: [K2tog] 8 times. (8 sts)

Break yarn and thread through rem sts. Pull tight and fasten off.

Legs

(make 2)

Using Candyfloss, cast on 10 sts.

Rows 1–24: St st 24 rows.

Cast (bind) off.

A

B

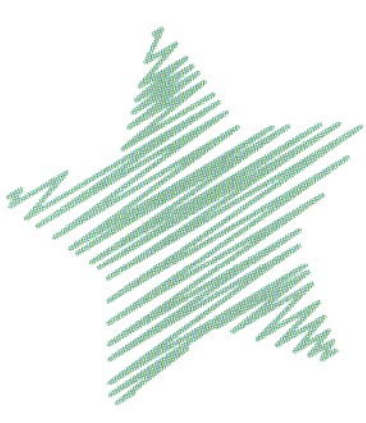

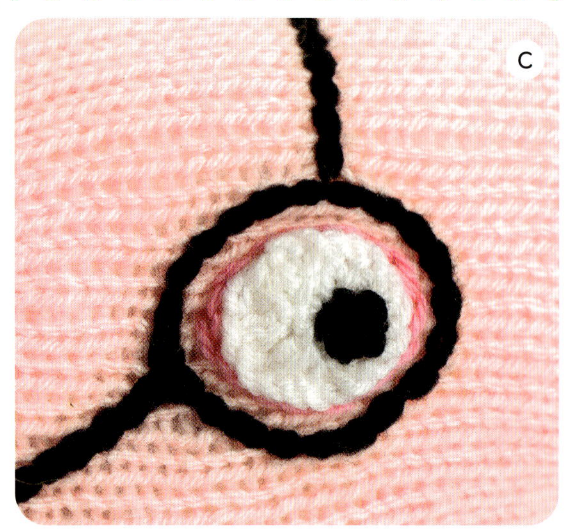

Shoes

(make 2)

Using Black, cast on 8 sts.

Row 1: [Kfb] 8 times. (16 sts)

Rows 2–16: Starting with a p row, st st 14 rows.

Row 17: [K2tog] 8 times. (8 sts)

Break yarn and thread through rem sts. Pull tight and fasten off.

Assembly

Sew all seams using mattress stitch (see Techniques: Sewing Up).

Join side seam of head and stuff. Join edges of each cheek to make a circle, then sew cheeks to face using photo as a guide for position. Join edges of each eye to make a circle, then sew each eye above a cheek. Using black embroidery thread (floss) and satin stitch (see Techniques: Satin Stitch), sew a pupil in each eye turned towards snout. Using Fondant, sew an outline around each eye using chain stitch (see Techniques: Chain Stitch), and then add an additional circle around each eye in Black for glasses **(C)**. Embroider a line to join both circles across bridge of nose and lines for arms of glasses towards back of head. Embroider a curved smile in straight stitch (see Techniques: Straight Stitch) below snout using Raspberry, then work back to fill gaps between stitches for a solid line **(D)**. Embroider nostrils in satin stitch at end of snout using Raspberry. For beard, embroider 4 stitches above smile and 6 sts below using Gingerbread **(D)**. Fold ears in half, sew side seam and then secure each ear to top of head on either side.

Join side seam of body and stuff. Position head on cast-on edge of body, with snout slightly tilted upwards, and sew in place.

Sew side seams of arms and each finger. Sew two fingers on either side of end on each arm. Sew an arm on each side of body, using the photo as a guide for position. Sew side seams of legs and shoes. Stuff shoes lightly, then gather cast-on edge to close. Sew a shoe to bottom of each leg, then sew each leg to bottom of body. Sew tail to centre back at bottom of body.

Weave in all ends (see Techniques: Weaving in Ends).

Granny Pig

Granny Pig is Mummy Pig's mum. She bakes delicious homemade chocolate cake and likes listening to rock and roll. She has a few chickens, and Peppa and George help feed them when they visit. She even enjoys doing historical reenactments with her friends.

Finished size

32cm (12½in)

Needles

3.5mm (US size 4) straight needles

Other tools and materials

- Toy stuffing
- Small amount of black embroidery thread (floss)
- Tapestry needle

Yarn

Samples are made with Stylecraft Special DK (100% acrylic), DK (light worsted) weight, 295m (322yd) per 100g (3½oz) ball in the following shades:

- 50g Powder Pink (1843)
- 35g White (1001)
- 5g Pale Rose (1080)
- 10g Black (1002)
- 35g Raspberry (1023)

Head

Start from back of head. Using Powder Pink, cast on 16 sts.

Row 1: [Kfb, k1] 8 times. (24 sts)

Row 2 and all even rows: P.

Row 3: [K1, kfb, k1] 8 times. (32 sts)

Row 5: [K2, kfb, k1] 8 times. (40 sts)

Row 7: [K3, kfb, k1] 8 times. (48 sts)

Row 9: [K4, kfb, k1] 8 times. (56 sts)

Row 11: [K5, kfb, k1] 8 times. (64 sts)

Rows 12–36: Starting with a p row, st st 25 rows.

Row 37: K1, ssk, k to last 3 sts, k2tog, k1. (62 sts)

Row 38: P.

Rows 39–52: Rep Rows 37 and 38. (48 sts)

Row 53: Cast (bind) off 2 sts, k to end. (46 sts)

Row 54: Cast (bind) off 2 sts, p to end. (44 sts)

Row 55: Cast (bind) off 2, sts, k to end. (42 sts)

Row 56: Cast (bind) off 2 sts, p to end. (40 sts)

Rows 57 and 58: K two rows.

Row 59: [K2, k2tog, k1] 8 times. (32 sts)

Row 61: [K1, k2tog, k1] 8 times. (24 sts)

Row 63: [K2tog, k1] 8 times. (16 sts)

Row 65: [K2tog] 8 times. (8 sts)

Break yarn and thread through rem sts. Pull tight and fasten off **(A)**.

Body

Start from neck. Using Powder Pink, cast on 32 sts.

Row 1: [K2, kfb, k1] 8 times. (40 sts)

Row 2 and all even rows: P.

Row 3: [K3, kfb, k1] 8 times. (48 sts)

Row 5: [K4, kfb, k1] 8 times. (56 sts)

Row 7: [K5, kfb, k1] 8 times. (64 sts)

Rows 8–32: Starting with a p row, st st 25 rows.

Row 33: [K5, k2tog, k1] 8 times. (56 sts)

Row 35: [K4, k2tog, k1] 8 times. (48 sts)

Row 37: [K3, k2tog, k1] 8 times. (40 sts)

Row 39: [K2, k2tog, k1] 8 times. (32 sts)

Row 41: [K1, k2tog, k1] 8 times. (24 sts)

Row 43: [K2tog, k1] 8 times. (16 sts)

Row 45: [K2tog] 8 times. (8 sts)

Break yarn and thread through rem sts. Pull tight and fasten off.

Arms

(make two)

Using Powder Pink, cast on 5 sts.

Row 1: K.

Row 2: Cast on 2 sts, p to end. (7 sts)

Row 3: Cast on 2 sts, k to end. (9 sts)

Rows 4–28: Starting with a p row, st st 25 rows.

Row 29: K1, [k2tog] 4 times. (5 sts)

Break yarn and thread through rem sts. Pull tight and fasten off.

Fingers

(make 2 per arm)

Using Powder Pink, cast on 5 sts.

Row 1: K.

Row 2: Cast on 2 sts, p to end. (7 sts)

Row 3: Cast on 2 sts, k to end. (9 sts)

Rows 4–6: Starting with a p row, st st 3 rows.

Row 7: K1, [k2tog] 4 times. (5 sts)

Break yarn and thread through rem sts. Pull tight and fasten off.

Ears

(make 2)

Using Powder Pink, cast on 20 sts.

Rows 1–10: Starting with a k row, st st 10 rows.

Row 11: [K2tog] 10 times. (10 sts)

Row 12: [P2tog] 5 times. (5 sts)

Break yarn and thread through rem sts. Pull tight and fasten off.

Tail

Using Powder Pink, cast on 25 sts.

Row 1: [Kfb] 25 times. (50 sts)

Cast (bind) off **(B)**.

Eyes

(make 2)

Using White cast on 20 sts.

Row 1: P.

Row 2: [K2tog] 10 times. (10 sts)

Row 3: [P2tog] 5 times. (5 sts)

Break yarn and thread through rem sts. Pull tight and fasten off.

Cheeks

(make 2)

Using Pale Rose, cast on 32 sts.

Row 1: P.

Row 2: [K2tog] 16 times. (16 sts)

Row 3: P.

Row 4: [K2tog] 8 times. (8 sts)

Break yarn and thread through rem sts. Pull tight and fasten off.

Legs

(make 2)

Using Powder Pink, cast on 10 sts.

Rows 1–24: St st 24 rows.

Cast (bind) off.

Shoes

(make 2)

Using Black, cast on 8 sts.

Row 1: [Kfb] 8 times. (16 sts)

Rows 2–16: Starting with a p row, st st 14 rows.

Row 17: [K2tog] 8 times. (8 sts)

Break yarn and thread through rem sts. Pull tight and fasten off.

A

B

Dress

Start from bottom of dress. Using Raspberry, cast on 80 sts.

Rows 1–4: G st 4 rows.

Rows 5–34: Starting with a k row, st st 30 rows.

Row 35: [K7, k2tog, k1] 8 times. (72 sts)

Row 36 and all even rows: P.

LEFT BACK

Work on first 18 sts only.

Row 37: [K6, k2tog, k1] 2 times. (16 sts)

Row 39: [K5, k2tog, k1] 2 times. (14 sts)

Row 41: [K4, k2tog, k1] 2 times. (12 sts)

Row 43: [K3, k2tog, k1] 2 times. (10 sts)

Break yarn.

FRONT

Rejoin yarn to centre sts, work next 36 sts only.

Row 37: [K6, k2tog, k1] 4 times. (32 sts)

Row 39: [K5, k2tog, k1] 4 times. (28 sts)

Row 41: [K4, k2tog, k1] 4 times. (24 sts)

Row 43: [K3, k2tog, k1] 4 times. (20 sts)

Break yarn.

RIGHT BACK

Rejoin yarn to last 18 sts, rep Rows 37–43 of left back.

Row 44: K10, join and k 20 sts for front, join and k last 10 sts. (40 sts)

Cast (bind) off knitwise.

Hat

Using White, cast on 56 sts.

Row 1: [K5, kfb, k1] 8 times. (64 sts)

Row 2 and all even rows: P.

Row 3: [K6, kfb, k1] 8 times. (72 sts)

Row 5: [K7, kfb, k1] 8 times. (80 sts)

Row 7: [K8, kfb, k1] 8 times. (88 sts)

Row 9: [K9, kfb, k1] 8 times. (96 sts)

Row 11: [K10, kfb, k1] 8 times. (104 sts)

Row 13: [K11, kfb, k1] 8 times. (112 sts)

Row 15: [K12, kfb, k1] 8 times. (120 sts)

Row 17: [K13, kfb, k1] 8 times. (128 sts)

Row 19: [K14, kfb, k1] 8 times. (136 sts)

Rows 20–22: Starting with a p row, st st 3 rows.

Row 23: [K14, k2tog, k1] 8 times. (128 sts)

Row 25: [K13, k2tog, k1] 8 times. (120 sts)

Row 27: [K12, k2tog, k1] 8 times. (112 sts)

Row 29: [K11, k2tog, k1] 8 times. (104 sts)

Row 31: [K10, k2tog, k1] 8 times. (96 sts)

Row 33: [K9, k2tog, k1] 8 times. (88 sts)

Row 35: [K8, k2tog, k1] 8 times. (80 sts)

Row 37: [K7, k2tog, k1] 8 times. (72 sts)

Row 39: [K6, k2tog, k1] 8 times. (64 sts)

Row 41: [K5, k2tog, k1] 8 times. (56 sts)

Rows 42–47: Change to Raspberry, starting with a p row, st st 6 rows.

Rows 48–58: Change to White, starting with a p row, st st 11 rows.

Row 59: [K4, k2tog, k1] 8 times. (48 sts)
Row 61: [K3, k2tog, k1] 8 times. (40 sts)
Row 63: [K2, k2tog, k1] 8 times. (32 sts)
Row 65: [K1, k2tog, k1] 8 times. (24 sts)
Row 67: [K2tog, k1] 8 times. (16 sts)
Row 68: [P2tog] 8 times. (8 sts)

Break off yarn and thread through rem sts.

Pull tight and fasten off **(C)**.

Assembly

Sew all seams using mattress stitch (see Techniques: Sewing Up).

Join side seam of head and stuff. Join edges of each cheek to make a circle, then sew cheeks to face using photo as a guide for position. Join edges of each eye to make a circle, then sew each eye above a cheek. Using black embroidery thread (floss) and satin stitch (see Techniques: Satin Stitch), sew a pupil in each eye turned towards snout. Using Pale Rose, sew an outline around each eye using chain stitch (see Techniques: Chain Stitch) and add eyelashes using White. Embroider a curved smile in straight stitch (see Techniques: Straight Stitch) below snout using Raspberry, then work back to fill gaps between stitches for a solid line. Embroider nostrils in satin stitch using Raspberry. Fold ears in half, sew side seam and then sew each ear to top of head on either side.

Join side seam of body and stuff. Position head on cast-on edge of body and sew in place. Place dress on body then sew side seam, leaving small gap for tail.

Sew side seams of arms and each finger. Sew two fingers on either side of end on each arm **(D)**. Sew side seams of legs and shoes. Stuff shoes lightly, then gather cast-on edge to close. Secure a shoe to bottom of each leg. Sew legs to bottom of body **(E)**. Using openings in dress as a guide, sew arms and tail to body.

Sew side seam of hat. Fold first twenty rows inwards and secure to rim of hat using running stitch. Stuff hat and then sew to top of head.

Weave in all ends (see Techniques: Weaving in Ends).

C

D

E

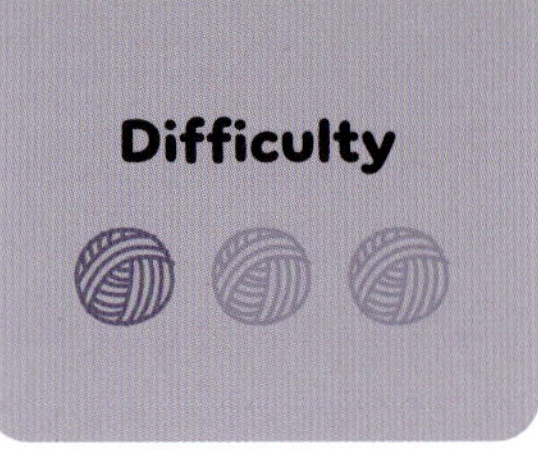

Grandpa Pig

Grandpa Pig is Mummy Pig's dad. He enjoys making things and is always taking on new adventures. He built a little train, named Gertrude, and takes Peppa and George for rides. He owns his own boat and loves sailing. Grandpa Pig is also very good at growing vegetables and takes pride in his garden.

Finished size

32cm (12½in)

Needles

3.5mm (US size 4) straight needles

Other tools and materials

- Toy stuffing
- Small amount of black embroidery thread (floss)
- Tapestry needle

Yarn

Samples are made with Stylecraft Special DK (100% acrylic), DK (light worsted) weight, 295m (322yd) per 100g (3½oz) ball in the following shades:

- 40g Powder Pink (1843)
- 25g Violet (1277)
- 5g White (1001)
- 10g Pale Rose (1080)
- 15g Black (1002)
- 5g Raspberry (1023)
- 5g Parma Violet (1724)

Head

Start from back of head. Using Powder Pink, Cast on 16 sts.

Row 1: [Kfb, k1] 8 times. (24 sts)

Row 2 and all even rows: P.

Row 3: [K1, kfb, k1] 8 times. (32 sts)

Row 5: [K2, kfb, k1] 8 times. (40 sts)

Row 7: [K3, kfb, k1] 8 times. (48 sts)

Row 9: [K4, kfb, k1] 8 times. (56 sts)

Row 11: [K5, kfb, k1] 8 times. (64 sts)

Rows 12–36: Starting with a p row, st st 25 rows.

Row 37: K1, ssk, k to last 3 sts, k2tog, k1. (62 sts)

Row 38: P.

Rows 39–52: Rep Rows 37 and 38. (48 sts)

Row 53: Cast (bind) off 2 sts, k to end. (46 sts)

Row 54: Cast (bind) off 2 sts, p to end. (44 sts)

Row 55: Cast (bind) off 2, sts, k to end. (32 sts)

Row 56: Cast (bind) off 2 sts, p to end. (40 sts)

Rows 57 and 58: K two rows.

Row 59: [K2, k2tog, k1] 8 times. (32 sts)

Row 61: [K1, k2tog, k1] 8 times. (24 sts)

Row 63: [K2tog, k1] 8 times. (16 sts)

Row 65: [K2tog] 8 times. (8 sts)

Break yarn and thread through rem sts. Pull tight and fasten off **(A)**.

Body

Start from neck. Using Violet, cast on 32 sts.

Row 1: [K2, kfb, k1] 8 times. (40 sts)

Row 2 and all even rows: P.

Row 3: [K3, kfb, k1] 8 times. (48 sts)

Row 5: [K4, kfb, k1] 8 times. (56 sts)

Row 7: [K5, kfb, k1] 8 times. (64 sts)

Rows 8–32: Starting with a p row, st st 25 rows.

Row 33: [K5, k2tog, k1] 8 times. (56 sts)

Row 35: [K4, k2tog, k1] 8 times. (48 sts)

Row 37: [K3, k2tog, k1] 8 times. (40 sts)

Row 39: [K2, k2tog, k1] 8 times. (32 sts)

Row 41: [K1, k2tog, k1] 8 times. (24 sts)

Row 43: [K2tog, k1] 8 times. (16 sts)

Row 45: [K2tog] 8 times. (8 sts)

Break yarn and thread through rem sts. Pull tight and fasten off.

Arms

(make two)

Using Powder Pink, cast on 5 sts.

Row 1: K.

Row 2: Cast on 2 sts, p to end. (7 sts)

Row 3: Cast on 2 sts, k to end. (9 sts)

Rows 4–28: Starting with a p row, st st 25 rows.

Row 29: K1, [k2tog] 4 times. (5 sts)

Break yarn and thread through rem sts. Pull tight and fasten off.

Fingers

(make 2 per arm)

Using Powder Pink, cast on 5 sts.

Row 1: K.

Row 2: Cast on 2 sts, p to end. (7 sts)

Row 3: Cast on 2 sts, k to end. (9 sts)

Rows 4–6: Starting with a p row, st st 3 rows.

Row 7: K1, [k2tog] 4 times. (5 sts)

Break yarn and thread through rem sts. Pull tight and fasten off.

Ears

(make 2)

Using Powder Pink, cast on 20 sts.

Rows 1–10: Starting with a k row, st st 10 rows.

Row 11: [K2tog] 10 times. (10 sts)

Row 12: [P2tog] 5 times. (5 sts)

Break yarn and thread through rem sts. Pull tight and fasten off.

Tail

Using Powder Pink, cast on 25 sts.

Row 1: [Kfb] 25 times. (50 sts)

Cast (bind) off.

Eyes

(make 2)

Using White, cast on 20 sts.

Row 1: P.

Row 2: [K2tog] 10 times. (10 sts)

Row 3: [P2tog] 5 times. (5 sts)

Break yarn and thread through rem sts. Pull tight and fasten off.

Cheeks

(make 2)

Using Pale Rose, cast on 32 sts.

Row 1: P.

Row 2: [K2tog] 16 times. (16 sts)

Row 3: P.

Row 4: [K2tog] 8 times. (8 sts)

Break yarn and thread through rem sts. Pull tight and fasten off.

Legs

(make 2)

Using Powder Pink, cast on 10 sts.

Rows 1–24: St st 24 rows.

Cast (bind) off **(B)**.

Shoes

(make 2)

Using Black, cast on 8 sts.

Row 1: [Kfb] 8 times. (16 sts)

Rows 2–16: Starting with a p row, st st 14 rows.

Row 17: [K2tog] 8 times. (8 sts)

Break yarn and thread through rem sts. Pull tight and fasten off **(B)**.

A

B

Hat

Using Violet, cast on 24 sts.

Rows 1 and 2: Starting with a k row, st st 2 rows.

Row 3: [K2tog] 2 times, k16, [k2tog] 2 times. (20 sts)

Row 4 and all even rows: P.

Row 5: [K2tog] 2 times, k12, [k2tog] 2 times. (16 sts)

Row 7: [K2tog] 2 times, k8, [k2tog] 2 times. (12 sts)

Rows 8–10: Starting with a p row, st st 3 rows.

Row 11: [Kfb] 2 times, k8, [kfb] 2 times. (16 sts)

Row 13: [Kfb] 2 times, k12, [kfb] 2 times. (20 sts)

Row 15: [Kfb] 2 times, k16, [kfb] 2 times. (24 sts)

Row 17: Cast on 16 sts, k to end. (40 sts)

Row 18: Cast on 16 sts, p to end. (56 sts)

Rows 19–30: Starting with a k row, st st 12 rows.

Row 31: [K4, k2tog, k1] 8 times. (48 sts)

Row 33: [K3, k2tog, k1] 8 times. (40 sts)

Row 35: [K2, k2tog, k1] 8 times. (32 sts)

Row 37: [K1, k2tog, k1] 8 times. (24 sts)

Row 39: [K2tog, k1] 8 times. (16 sts)

Row 41: [P2tog] 8 times. (8 sts)

Break yarn and thread through rem sts. Pull tight and fasten off **(C)**.

Hat embroidery chart

Each square represents one stitch.

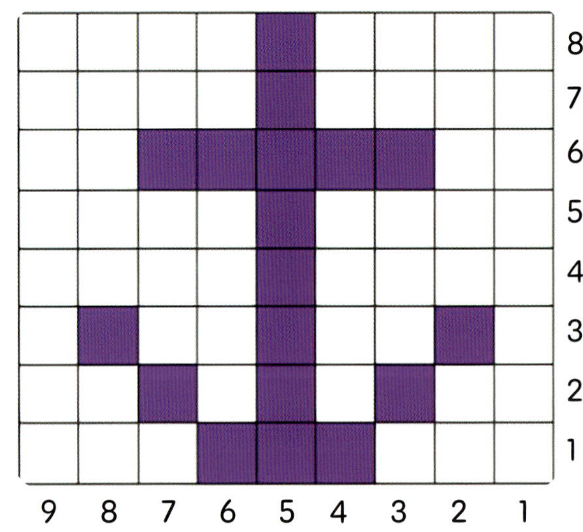

Assembly

Sew all seams using mattress stitch (see Techniques: Sewing Up).

Join side seam of head and stuff. Join edges of each cheek to make a circle, then sew cheeks to face using photo as a guide for position. Join edges of each eye to make a circle, then sew each eye above a cheek. Using black embroidery thread (floss) and satin stitch (see Techniques: Satin Stitch), sew a pupil in each eye. Using Pale Rose, sew an outline around each eye using chain stitch (see Techniques: Chain Stitch). Embroider a curved smile in straight stitch (see Techniques: Straight Stitch) below snout using Raspberry, then work back to fill gaps between stitches for a solid line **(D)**. Embroider nostrils in satin stitch using Raspberry. For beard, embroider three lines above mouth and four lines below using White **(D)**. Fold ears in half, sew side seam and then secure each ear to top of head on either side.

Join side seam of body and stuff. Position head on cast-on edge of body and sew in place.

Sew side seams of arms and each finger. Sew two fingers on either side of end on each arm. Sew an arm on each side of body, using the photo as a guide for position. Sew side seams of legs and shoes. Stuff shoes lightly, then gather cast-on edge to close. Sew a shoe to bottom of each leg, then sew each leg to bottom of body. Sew tail to centre back at bottom of body.

Sew side seam of hat and then sew flap inwards and secure with running stitch. Using Parma Violet sew anchor on hat in duplicate stitch (see Techniques: Duplicate Stitch) **(E)**. Block hat, ensuring rim is tucked inwards. Stuff hat and then sew to top of head.

Weave in all ends (see Techniques: Weaving in Ends).

E

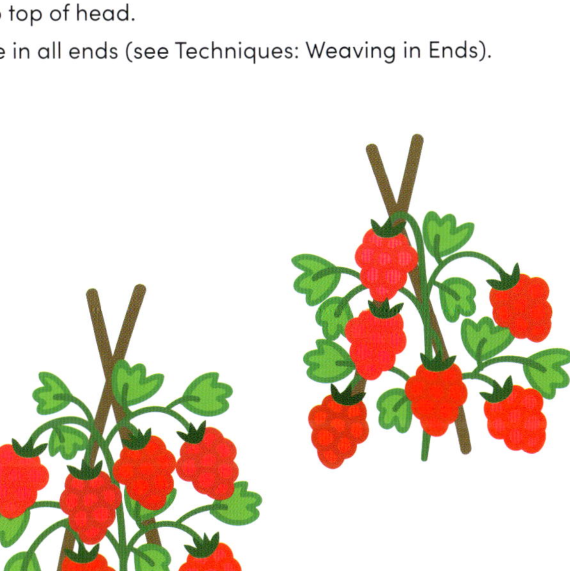

Difficulty

Suzy Sheep

Suzy Sheep has been Peppa's best friend ever since they were babies, even their mummies are best friends. Suzy is very confident and enjoys playing sports. She loves dress-up and wants to be a nurse when she grows up so she can help people.

Finished size

26cm (10¼in)

Needles

3.5mm (US size 4) straight needles

Other tools and materials

- Large fork or 3.5–4cm (1½in) pompom maker
- Toy stuffing
- Small amount of black embroidery thread (floss)
- Tapestry needle

Yarn

Samples are made with Stylecraft Special DK (100% acrylic), DK (light worsted) weight, 295m (322yd) per 100g (3½oz) ball in the following shades:

- 35g White (1001)
- 20g Fondant (1241)
- 10g Candyfloss (1130)
- 10g Black (1002)
- 5g Silver (1203)
- 5g Bright Pink (1435)

Head

Start from neck. Using White, cast on 16 sts.

Row 1: [Kfb, k1] 8 times. (24 sts)

Row 2 and all even rows: P.

Row 3: [K1, kfb, k1] 8 times.(32 sts)

Row 5: [K2, kfb, k1] 8 times. (40 sts)

Row 7: [K3, kfb, k1] 8 times. (48 sts)

Row 9: [K4, kfb, k1] 8 times. (56 sts)

Row 11: [K5, kfb, k1] 8 times. (64 sts)

Rows 12–28: Starting with a p row, st st 17 rows.

Row 29: [K5, k2tog, k1] 8 times. (56 sts)

Rows 30–32: Starting with a p row, st st 3 rows.

Row 33: [K4, k2tog, k1] 8 times. (48 sts)

Rows 34–36: Starting with a p row, st st 3 rows.

Row 37: [K3, k2tog, k1] 8 times. (40 sts)

Rows 38–40: Starting with a p row, st st 3 rows.

Row 41: [K2, k2tog, k1] 8 times. (32 sts)

Rows 42–44: Starting with a p row, st st 3 rows.

Row 45: [K1, k2tog, k1] 8 times. (24 sts)

Row 47: [K2tog, k1] 8 times. (16 sts)

Row 49: [K2tog] 8 times. (8 sts)

Break yarn and thread through rem sts. Pull tight and fasten off.

Body

Start from neck. Using White, cast on 24 sts.

Rows 1 and 2: Starting with a k row, st st 2 rows.

Row 3: [K1, kfb, k1] 8 times. (32 sts)

Row 4 and all even rows: P.

Row 5: [K2, kfb, k1] 8 times. (40 sts)

Row 7: [K3, kfb, k1] 8 times. (48 sts)

Row 9: [K4, kfb, k1] 8 times. (56 sts)

Rows 10–28: Starting with a p row, st st 19 rows.

Row 29: [K4, k2tog, k1] 8 times. (48 sts)

Row 31: [K3, k2tog, k1] 8 times. (40 sts)

Row 33: [K2, k2tog, k1] 8 times. (32 sts)

Row 35: [K1, k2tog, k1] 8 times. (24 sts)

Row 37: [K2tog, k1] 8 times. (16 sts)

Row 39: [K2tog] 8 times. (8 sts)

Break yarn and thread through rem sts. Pull tight and fasten off.

Arms

(make 2)

Using White, cast on 5 sts.

Row 1: K.

Row 2: Cast on 2 sts, p to end. (7 sts)

Row 3: Cast on 2 sts, k to end. (9 sts)

Rows 4–24: Starting with a p row, st st 21 rows.

Row 25: K1, [k2tog] 4 times. (5 sts)

Break yarn and thread through rem sts. Pull tight and fasten off.

Fingers

(make 2 per arm)

Using White, cast on 5 sts.

Row 1: K.

Row 2: Cast on 2 sts, p to end. (7 sts)

Row 3: Cast on 2 sts, k to end. (9 sts)

Rows 4–6: Starting with a p row, st st 3 rows.

Row 7: K1, [k2tog] 4 times. (5 sts)

Break yarn and thread through rem sts. Pull tight and fasten off.

Ears

(make 2)

Using White, cast on 18 sts.

Rows 1–6: Starting with a k row, st st 6 rows.

Row 7: [K2tog, k1] 6 times. (12 sts)

Row 8: P.

Row 9: [K2tog] 6 times. (6 sts)

Break yarn and thread through rem sts. Pull tight and fasten off.

Nose

Using Fondant, cast on 16 sts.

Row 1: [Kfb, k1] 8 times. (24 sts)

Rows 2–6: Starting with a p row, st st 5 rows.

Row 7: [K2tog, k1] 8 times. (16 sts)

Row 8: P.

Row 9: [K2tog] 8 times. (8 sts)

Break yarn and thread through rem sts. Pull tight and fasten off **(A)**.

Tail

Make a small pompom (see Techniques: Making a Tiny Pompom) using White. Leave a long end for sewing to body **(B)**.

Eyes

(make 2)

Using White, cast on 14 sts.

Row 1: P.

Row 2: [K2tog] 7 times. (7 sts)

Break yarn and thread through rem sts. Pull tight and fasten off.

Cheeks

(make 2)

Using Candyfloss, cast on 28 sts.

Row 1: P.

Row 2: [K2tog] 14 times. (14 sts)

Row 3: [P2tog] 7 times. (7 sts)

Break yarn and thread through rem sts. Pull tight and fasten off.

Legs

(make 2)

Using White, cast on 10 sts.

Rows 1–19: Starting with a k row, st st 19 rows.

Cast (bind) off **(C)**.

Shoes

(make 2)

Using Black, cast on 6 sts.

Row 1: [Kfb] 6 times. (12 sts)

Rows 2–14: Starting with a p row, st st 13 rows.

Row 15: [K2tog] 6 times. (6 sts)

Break yarn and thread through rem sts. Pull tight and fasten off **(C)**.

Dress

Start from bottom of dress. Using Fondant, cast on 72 sts.

Rows 1–4: G st 4 rows.

Rows 5–24: Starting with a k row, st st 20 rows.

Row 25: [K6, k2tog, k1] 8 times. (64 sts)

Row 26 and all even rows: P.

LEFT BACK

Work on first 16 sts only.

Row 27: [K5, k2tog, k1] 2 times. (14 sts)

Row 29: [K4, k2tog, k1] 2 times. (12 sts)

Row 31: [K3, k2tog, k1] 2 times. (10 sts)

Row 33: [K2, k2tog, k1] 2 times. (8 sts)

Break yarn.

FRONT

Rejoin yarn to centre 32 sts, work these 32 sts only.

Row 27: [K5, k2tog, k1] 4 times. (28 sts)

Row 29: [K4, k2tog, k1] 4 times. (24 sts)

Row 31: [K3, k2tog, k1] 4 times. (20 sts)

Row 33: [K2, k2tog, k1] 4 times. (16 sts)

Break yarn.

RIGHT BACK

Rejoin yarn to last 16 sts and rep Rows 27–33 of left back.

Row 34: K8, join and k 16 sts for front, then join and k last 8 sts. (32 sts)

Cast (bind) off knitwise.

Assembly

Sew all seams using mattress stitch (see Techniques: Sewing Up).

Join side seam of head and stuff. Sew side seam of nose and stuff, then sew nose to head using photo as a guide for position. Join edges of each cheek to make a circle, then sew cheeks to either side of face. Join edges of each eye to make a circle, then sew each eye above a cheek **(D)**. Using black embroidery thread (floss) and satin stitch (see Techniques: Satin Stitch), sew a pupil in each eye. Using Silver, sew an outline around each eye using chain stitch (see Techniques: Chain Stitch). Embroider a curved smile in straight stitch (see Techniques: Straight Stitch) using Bright Pink **(E)**, then work back to fill gaps between stitches for a solid line. Fold ears in half, sew side seam and then secure each ear to top of head on either side.

Join side seam of body and stuff. Position head on cast-on edge of body and sew in place. Place dress on body then sew side seam, leaving small gap for tail.

Sew side seams of arms and each finger. Sew two fingers on either side of end on each arm. Sew side seams of legs and shoes. Stuff shoes lightly, then gather cast-on edge to close. Secure a shoe to bottom of each leg. Sew legs to bottom of body. Using openings in dress as a guide, sew arms and tail to body.

Weave in all ends (see Techniques: Weaving in Ends).

D

E

Difficulty

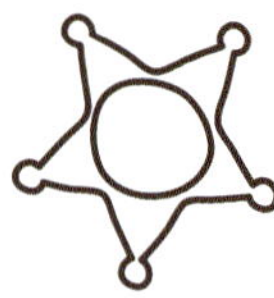

Pedro Pony

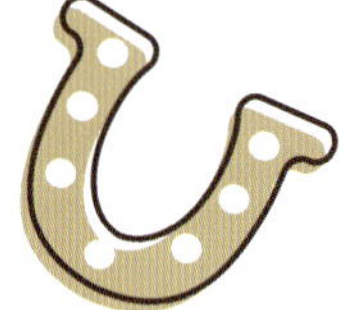

Pedro Pony is one of Peppa's playgroup friends. His dad is Mr. Pony, an optician. Pedro loves cowboys, dress-up, and being outdoors. He has many talents, including magic tricks and playing the ukulele. Pedro also has a pet stick insect named Steven.

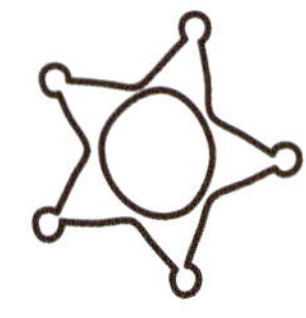

Finished size

28cm (11in)

Needles

3.5mm (US size 4) straight needles

Other tools and materials

- Toy stuffing
- Small amount of black embroidery thread (floss)
- Tapestry needle

Yarn

Samples are made with Stylecraft Special DK (100% acrylic), DK (light worsted) weight, 295m (322yd) per 100g (3½oz) ball in the following shades:

- 35g Camel (1420)
- 20g Pistachio (1822)
- 10g White (1001)
- 15g Toy (1844)
- 5g Fondant (1241)
- 10g Black (1002)
- 5g Mocha (1064)
- 5g Raspberry (1023)

Head

Start from neck. Using Camel, cast on 16 sts.

Row 1: [Kfb, k1] 8 times. (24 sts)

Row 2 and all even rows: P.

Row 3: [K1, kfb, k1] 8 times. (32 sts)

Row 5: [K2, kfb, k1] 8 times. (40 sts)

Row 7: [K3, kfb, k1] 8 times. (48 sts)

Row 9: [K4, kfb, k1] 8 times. (56 sts)

Row 11: [K5, kfb, k1] 8 times. (64 sts)

Rows 12–34: Starting with a p row, st st 23 rows.

Row 35: [K5, k2tog, k1] 8 times. (56 sts)

Row 37: [K4, k2tog, k1] 8 times. (48 sts)

Row 39: [K3, k2tog, k1] 8 times. (40 sts)

Row 41: [K2, k2tog, k1] 8 times. (32 sts)

Break Camel, join in Fondant.

Rows 42–44: P 3 rows.

Row 45: K4, [k2tog] 4 times, k8, [k2tog] 4 times, k4. (24 sts)

Row 47: K2, [k2tog] 4 times, k4, [k2tog] 4 times, k2. (16 sts)

Row 49: [K2tog] 8 times. (8 sts)

Break yarn and thread through rem sts. Pull tight and fasten off **(A)**.

Body

Start from neck. Using Pistachio, cast on 24 sts.

Rows 1 and 2: Starting with a k row, st st 2 rows.

Row 3: [K1, kfb, k1] 8 times. (32 sts)

Row 4 and all even rows: P.

Row 5: [K2, kfb, k1] 8 times. (40 sts)

Row 7: [K3, kfb, k1] 8 times. (48 sts)

Row 9: [K4, kfb, k1] 8 times. (56 sts)

Rows 10–28: Starting with a p row, st st 19 rows.

Row 29: [K4, k2tog, k1] 8 times. (48 sts)

Row 31: [K3, k2tog, k1] 8 times. (40 sts)

Row 33: [K2, k2tog, k1] 8 times. (32 sts)

Row 35: [K1, k2tog, k1] 8 times. (24 sts)

Row 37: [K2tog, k1] 8 times. (16 sts)

Row 39: [K2tog] 8 times. (8 sts)

Break yarn and thread through rem sts. Pull tight and fasten off.

Arms

(make 2)

Using Camel, cast on 5 sts.

Row 1: K.

Row 2: Cast on 2 sts, p to end. (7 sts)

Row 3: Cast on 2 sts, k to end. (9 sts)

Rows 4–24: Starting with a p row, st st 21 rows.

Row 25: K1, [k2tog] 4 times. (5 sts)

Break yarn and thread through rem sts. Pull tight and fasten off.

Fingers

(make 2 per arm)

Using Camel, cast on 5 sts.

Row 1: K.

Row 2: Cast on 2 sts, p to end. (7 sts)

Row 3: Cast on 2 sts, k to end. (9 sts)

Rows 4–6: Starting with a p row, st st 3 rows.

Row 7: K1, [k2tog] 4 times. (5 sts)

Break yarn and thread through rem sts. Pull tight and fasten off.

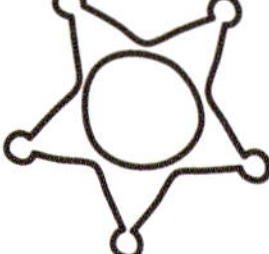

Ears

(make 2)

Using Camel, cast on 18 sts.

Rows 1–6: Starting with a k row, st st 6 rows.

Row 7: [K2tog, k1] 6 times. (12 sts)

Row 8: P.

Row 9: [K2tog] 6 times. (6 sts)

Break yarn and thread through rem sts. Pull tight and fasten off.

Tail

(make 3)

Using Camel, cast on 10 sts.

Rows 1–22: Starting with a k row, st st 22 rows.

Row 23: [K2tog] 5 times. (5 sts)

Break yarn and thread through rem sts. Pull tight and fasten off **(B)**.

Eyes

(make 2)

Using White, cast on 14 sts.

Row 1: P.

Row 2: [K2tog] 7 times. (7 sts)

Break yarn and thread through rem sts. Pull tight and fasten off.

A

B

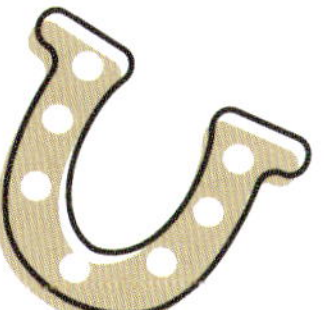

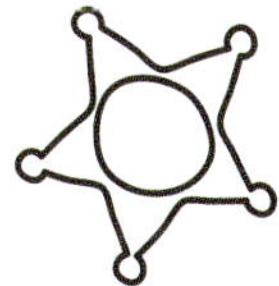

Spots

(make 8)

Using Toy, cast on 28 sts.

Row 1: P.

Row 2: [K2tog] 14 times. (14 sts)

Row 3: [P2tog] 7 times. (7 sts)

Break yarn and thread through rem sts. Pull tight and fasten off **(C)**.

Leg

(make 2)

Using Camel, cast on 10 sts.

Rows 1–19: Starting with a k row, st st 19 rows.

Cast (bind) off **(D)**.

Shoes

(make 2)

Using Black, cast on 6 sts.

Row 1: [Kfb] 6 times. (12 sts)

Rows 2–14: Starting with a p row, st st 13 rows.

Row 15: [K2tog] 6 times. (6 sts)

Break yarn and thread through rem sts. Pull tight and fasten off **(D)**.

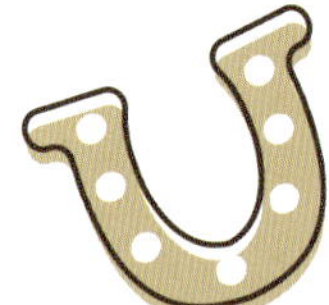

Assembly

Sew all seams using mattress stitch (see Techniques: Sewing Up).

Join side seam of head and stuff. Join edges of each eye to make a circle, then sew each eye onto face, using photo as a guide. Using black embroidery thread (floss) and satin stitch (see Techniques: Satin Stitch), sew a pupil in each eye. Using Black, sew an outline around each eye using chain stitch (see Techniques: Chain Stitch) for glasses, then connect two circles with a straight line of chain stitch across nose. Add a horizontal line from side of circle towards back on each side for glasses arms **(E)**. Embroider a curved smile in straight stitch (see Techniques: Straight Stitch) using Mocha, then work back to fill gaps between stitches for a solid line. Embroider nostrils in Raspberry. Join edges of each spot to make a circle, then sew four spots on each side of face using photo as a guide for position. Fold ears in half, sew side seam and then secure each ear to top of head on either side.

Join side seam of body and stuff. Position head on cast-on edge of body and sew in place. Sew side seams of arms and each finger. Sew two fingers on either side of end on each arm, then sew arms to either side of body. Sew side seam of tail and tail parts, then sew three tail parts vertically above one another to back. Sew side seams of legs and shoes. Stuff shoes lightly, then gather cast-on edge to close. Secure a shoe to bottom of each leg. Sew legs to bottom of body.

Weave in all ends (see Techniques: Weaving in Ends).

D

E

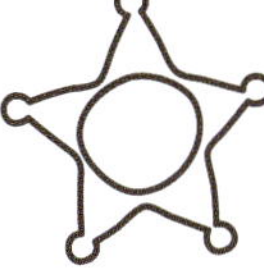

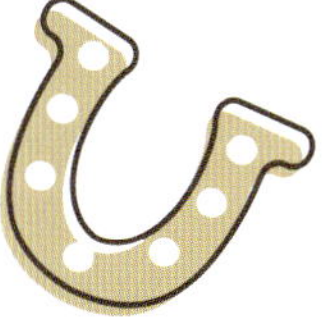

Difficulty

Rebecca Rabbit

Rebecca Rabbit lives in a burrow on a hill with her mummy, daddy, and siblings Richard, Robbie and Rosie. She is very caring and isn't afraid to stand up for what is right. She is a natural leader, like her friend Peppa. Rebecca enjoys swimming, riding her bike, and ballet. She is very good at hopping and really loves carrots.

Finished size

30cm (11¾in)

Needles

3.5mm (US size 4) straight needles

Other tools and materials

- Large fork or 3.5–4cm (1½in) pompom maker
- Toy stuffing
- Small amount of black embroidery thread (floss)
- Tapestry needle

Yarn

Samples are made with Stylecraft Special DK (100% acrylic), DK (light worsted) weight, 295m (322yd) per 100g (3½oz) ball in the following shades:

- 35g Cream (1005)
- 5g Fondant (1241)
- 10g White (1001)
- 10g Apricot (1026)
- 10g Black (1002)
- 20g Aspen (1422)
- 5g Parchment (1218)
- 5g Bright Pink (1435)

Head

Start from neck. Using Cream, cast on 16 sts.

Row 1: [Kfb, k1] 8 times. (24 sts)

Row 2 and all even rows: P.

Row 3: [K1, kfb, k1] 8 times. (32 sts)

Row 5: [K2, kfb, k1] 8 times. (40 sts)

Row 7: [K3, kfb, k1] 8 times. (48 sts)

Row 9: [K4, kfb, k1] 8 times. (56 sts)

Row 11: [K5, kfb, k1] 8 times. (64 sts)

Row 13: [K8, k2tog, k6] 4 times. (60 sts)

Rows 14–16: Starting with a p row, st st 3 rows.

Row 17: [K7, k2tog, k6] 4 times. (56 sts)

Rows 18–20: Starting with a p row, st st 3 rows.

Row 21: [K6, k2tog, k6] 4 times. (52 sts)

Rows 22–24: Starting with a p row, st st 3 rows.

Row 25: [K5, k2tog, k6] 4 times. (48 sts)

Rows 26–28: Starting with a p row, st st 3 rows.

Row 29: [K4, k2tog, k6] 4 times. (44 sts)

Rows 30–32: Starting with a p row, st st 3 rows.

Row 33: [K3, k2tog, k6] 4 times. (40 sts)

Rows 34–36: Starting with a p row, st st 3 rows.

Row 37: [K2, k2tog, k6] 4 times. (36 sts)

Rows 38–40: Starting with a p row, st st 3 rows.

Row 41: [K1, k2tog, k6] 4 times. (32 sts)

Rows 42–44: Starting with a p row, st st 3 rows.

Row 45: [K1, k2tog, k1] 8 times. (24 sts)

Row 47: [K2tog, k1] 8 times. (16 sts)

Row 49: [K2tog] 8 times. (8 sts)

Break yarn and thread through rem sts. Pull tight and fasten off.

Body

Start from neck. Using Cream, cast on 24 sts.

Rows 1 and 2: Starting with a k row, st st 2 rows.

Row 3: [K1, kfb, k1] 8 times. (32 sts)

Row 4 and all even rows: P.

Row 5: [K2, kfb, k1] 8 times. (40 sts)

Row 7: [K3, kfb, k1] 8 times. (48 sts)

Row 9: [K4, kfb, k1] 8 times. (56 sts)

Rows 10–28: Starting with a p row, st st 19 rows.

Row 29: [K4, k2tog, k1] 8 times. (48 sts)

Row 31: [K3, k2tog, k1] 8 times. (40 sts)

Row 33: [K2, k2tog, k1] 8 times. (32 sts)

Row 35: [K1, k2tog, k1] 8 times. (24 sts)

Row 37: [K2tog, k1] 8 times. (16 sts)

Row 39: [K2tog] 8 times. (8 sts)

Break yarn and thread through rem sts. Pull tight and fasten off.

Arms

(make 2)

Using Cream, cast on 5 sts.

Row 1: K.

Row 2: Cast on 2 sts, p to end. (7 sts)

Row 3: Cast on 2 sts, k to end. (9 sts)

Rows 4–24: Starting with a p row, st st 21 rows.

Row 25: K1, [k2tog] 4 times. (5 sts)

Break yarn and thread through rem sts. Pull tight and fasten off.

Fingers

(make 2 per arm)

Using Cream, cast on 5 sts.

Row 1: K.

Row 2: Cast on 2 sts, p to end. (7 sts)

Row 3: Cast on 2 sts, k to end. (9 sts)

Rows 4–6: Starting with a p row, st st 3 rows.

Row 7: K1, [k2tog] 4 times. (5 sts)

Break yarn and thread through rem sts. Pull tight and fasten off.

Ears

(make 2)

Using Cream, cast on 18 sts.

Rows 1–26: Starting with a k row, st st 26 rows.

Row 27: [K2tog, k1] 6 times. (12 sts)

Row 28: P.

Row 29: [K2tog] 6 times. (6 sts)

Break yarn and thread through rem sts. Pull tight and fasten off **(A)**.

Nose

Using Fondant, cast on 16 sts

Row 1: [Kfb, k1] 8 times. (24 sts)

Rows 2–6: Starting with a p row, st st 5 rows.

Row 7: [K2tog, k1] 8 times. (16 sts)

Row 8: P.

Row 9: [K2tog] 8 times. (8 sts)

Break yarn and thread through rem sts. Pull tight and fasten off **(B)**.

Tail

Make a small pompom (see Techniques: Making a Tiny Pompom) using White. Leave a long end for sewing to body.

Cheeks

(make 2)

Using Apricot, cast on 28 sts.

Row 1: P.

Row 2: [K2tog] 14 times. (14 sts)

Row 3: [P2tog] 7 times. (7 sts)

Break yarn and thread through rem sts. Pull tight and fasten off.

A

B

Legs

(make 2)

Using Cream, cast on 10 sts.

Rows 1–19: Starting with a k row, st st 19 rows.

Cast (bind) off **(C)**.

Shoes

(make 2)

Using Black, cast on 6 sts.

Row 1: [Kfb] 6 times. (12 sts)

Rows 2–14: Starting with a p row, st st 13 rows.

Row 15: [K2tog] 6 times. (6 sts)

Break yarn and thread through rem sts. Pull tight and fasten off **(C)**.

Dress

Start from bottom of dress. Using Aspen, cast on 72 sts.

Rows 1–4: G st 4 rows.

Rows 5–24: Starting with a k row, st st 20 rows.

Row 25: [K6, k2tog, k1] 8 times. (64 sts)

Row 26 and all even rows: P.

LEFT BACK

Work on first 16 sts only.

Row 27: [K5, k2tog, k1] 2 times. (14 sts)

Row 29: [K4, k2tog, k1] 2 times. (12 sts)

Row 31: [K3, k2tog, k1] 2 times. (10 sts)

Row 33: [K2, k2tog, k1] 2 times. (8 sts)

Break yarn.

FRONT

Rejoin yarn to centre 32 sts, work these 32 sts only.

Row 27: [K5, k2tog, k1] 4 times. (28 sts)

Row 29: [K4, k2tog, k1] 4 times. (24 sts)

Row 31: [K3, k2tog, k1] 4 times. (20 sts)

Row 33: [K2, k2tog, k1] 4 times. (16 sts)

Break yarn.

RIGHT BACK

Rejoin yarn to last 16 sts and rep Rows 27–33 of left back.

Row 34: K8, join and k 16 sts for front, then join and k last 8 sts. (32 sts)

Cast (bind) off knitwise.

Assembly

Sew all seams using mattress stitch (see Techniques: Sewing Up).

Join side seam of head and stuff. Sew side seam of nose and stuff, then sew nose to head using photo as a guide. Join edges of each cheek to make a circle, then sew cheeks to face on either side of nose. Join edges of each eye to make a circle, then sew each eye above a cheek. Using black embroidery thread (floss) and satin stitch (see Techniques: Satin Stitch), sew a pupil in each eye. Using Parchment, sew an outline around each eye using chain stitch (see Techniques: Chain Stitch). Embroider a curved smile in straight stitch (see Techniques: Straight Stitch) using Bright Pink, then work back to fill gaps between stitches for a solid line. Fold ears in half, sew side seam and then secure each ear to top of head on either side.

Join side seam of body and stuff. Position head on cast-on edge of body and sew in place. Place dress on body then sew side seam, leaving small gap for tail.

Sew side seams of arms and each finger. Sew two fingers on either side of end on each arm **(D)**. Sew side seams of legs and shoes. Stuff shoes lightly, then gather cast-on edge to close. Secure a shoe to bottom of each leg. Sew legs to bottom of body. Using openings in dress as a guide, sew arms and tail **(E)** to body.

Weave in all ends (see Techniques: Weaving in Ends).

E

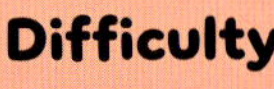

Difficulty

Danny Dog

Danny Dog is confident and outgoing. He enjoys being active, playing football, and pretending to be a pirate. He even has a pirate-themed bedroom. Danny Dog loves cars and helping Granddad Dog in his garage. When he grows up, he wants to be a sea captain, just like his dad.

Finished size

26cm (10¼in)

Needles

3.5mm (US size 4) straight needles

Other tools and materials

- Tapestry needle
- Small amount of black embroidery thread (floss)
- Toy stuffing

Yarn

Samples are made with Stylecraft Special DK (100% acrylic), DK (light worsted) weight, 295m (322yd) per 100g (3½oz) ball in the following shades:

- 35g Mocha (1064)
- 20g Proper Purple (1855)
- 10g Black (1002)
- 10g White (1001)
- 10g Copper (1029)
- 5g Walnut (1054)

Body

Start from neck. Using Proper Purple, cast on 24 sts.

Rows 1 and 2: Starting with a k row, st st 2 rows.

Row 3: [K1, kfb, k1] 8 times. (32 sts)

Row 4 and all even rows: P.

Row 5: [K2, kfb, k1] 8 times. (40 sts)

Row 7: [K3, kfb, k1] 8 times. (48 sts)

Row 9: [K4, kfb, k1] 8 times. (56 sts)

Rows 10–28: Starting with a p row, st st 19 rows.

Row 29: [K4, k2tog, k1] 8 times. (48 sts)

Row 31: [K3, k2tog, k1] 8 times. (40 sts)

Row 33: [K2, k2tog, k1] 8 times. (32 sts)

Row 35: [K1, k2tog, k1] 8 times. (24 sts)

Row 37: [K2tog, k1] 8 times. (16 sts)

Row 39: [K2tog] 8 times. (8 sts)

Break yarn and thread through rem sts. Pull tight and fasten off.

Head

Start from neck. Using Mocha, cast on 16 sts.

Row 1: [Kfb, k1] 8 times. (24 sts)

Row 2 and all even rows: P.

Row 3: [K1, kfb, k1] 8 times. (32 sts)

Row 5: [K2, kfb, k1] 8 times. (40 sts)

Row 7: [K3, kfb, k1] 8 times. (48 sts)

Row 9: [K4, kfb, k1] 8 times. (56 sts)

Row 11: [K5, kfb, k1] 8 times. (64 sts)

Rows 12–28: Starting with a p row, st st 17 rows.

Row 29: [K5, k2tog, k1] 8 times. (56 sts)

Rows 30–32: Starting with a p row, st st 3 rows.

Row 33: [K4, k2tog, k1] 8 times. (48 sts)

Rows 34–36: Starting with a p row, st st 3 rows.

Row 37: [K3, k2tog, k1] 8 times. (40 sts)

Rows 38–40: Starting with a p row, st st 3 rows.

Row 41: [K2, k2tog, k1] 8 times. (32 sts)

Rows 42–44: Starting with a p row, st st 3 rows.

Row 45: [K1, k2tog, k1] 8 times. (24 sts)

Row 47: [K2tog, k1] 8 times. (16 sts)

Row 49: [K2tog] 8 times. (8 sts)

Break yarn and thread through rem sts. Pull tight and fasten off **(A)**.

Arms

(make 2)

Using Mocha, cast on 5 sts.

Row 1: K.

Row 2: Cast on 2 sts, p to end. (7 sts)

Row 3: Cast on 2 sts, k to end. (9 sts)

Rows 4–24: Starting with a p row, st st 21 rows.

Row 25: K1, [k2tog] 4 times. (5 sts)

Break yarn and thread through rem sts. Pull tight and fasten off.

Fingers

(make 2 per arm)

Using Mocha, cast on 5 sts.

Row 1: K.

Row 2: Cast on 2 sts, p to end. (7 sts)

Row 3: Cast on 2 sts, k to end. (9 sts)

Rows 4–6: Starting with a p row, st st 3 rows.

Row 7: K1, [k2tog] 4 times. (5 sts)

Break yarn and thread through rem sts. Pull tight and fasten off.

Nose

Using Black, cast on 32 sts.

Rows 1–4: Starting with a k row, st st 4 rows.

Row 5: [K1, k2tog, k1] 8 times. (24 sts)

Row 6 and all even rows: P.

Row 7: [K2tog, k1] 8 times. (16 sts)

Row 9: [K2tog] 8 times. (8 sts)

Break yarn and thread through rem sts. Pull tight and fasten off.

Ears

(make two)

Using Mocha, cast on 24 sts.

Rows 1 and 2: Starting with a k row, st st 2 rows.

Row 3: [K1, k2tog, k6, k2tog, k1] 2 times. (20 sts)

Row 4 and all even rows: P.

Row 5: [K1, k2tog, k4, k2tog, k1] 2 times. (16 sts)

Row 7: [K1, k2tog, k2, k2tog, k1] 2 times. (12 sts)

Row 9: [K1, k2tog, k2tog, k1] 2 times. (8 sts)

Row 11: [K2tog] 4 times. (4 sts)

Row 12: [P2tog] 2 times. (2 sts)

Break yarn and thread through rem sts. Pull tight and fasten off **(B)**.

Tail

Using Mocha, cast on 10 sts.

Rows 1–22: Starting with a k row, st st 22 rows.

Row 23: [K2tog] 5 times. (5 sts)

Break yarn and thread through rem sts. Pull tight and fasten off.

Eyes

(make 2)

Using White, cast on 14 sts.

Row 1: P.

Row 2: [K2tog] 7 times. (7 sts)

Break yarn and thread through rem sts. Pull tight and fasten off **(C)**.

Cheeks

(make 2)

Using Copper, cast on 28 sts.

Row 1: P.

Row 2: [K2tog] 14 times. (14 sts)

Row 3: [P2tog] 7 times. (7 sts)

Break yarn and thread through rem sts. Pull tight and fasten off **(C)**.

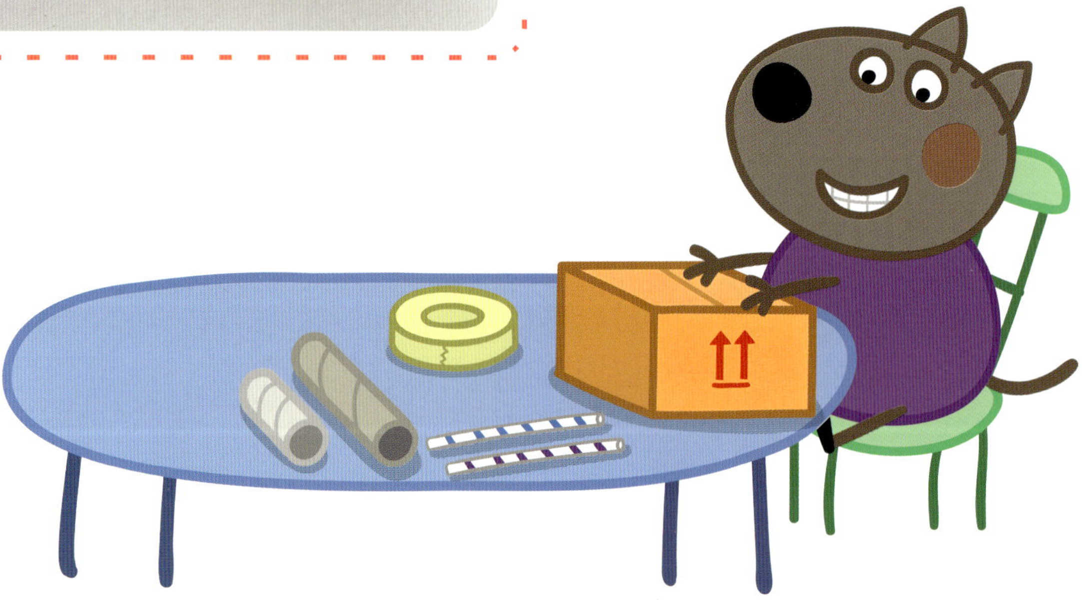

Legs

(make 2)

Using Mocha, cast on 10 sts.

Rows 1–19: Starting with a k row, st st 19 rows.

Cast (bind) off **(D)**.

Shoes

(make 2)

Using Black, cast on 6 sts.

Row 1: [Kfb] 6 times. (12 sts)

Rows 2–14: Starting with a p row, st st 13 rows.

Row 15: [K2tog] 6 times. (6 sts)

Break yarn and thread through rem sts.

Pull tight and fasten off **(D)**.

Assembly

Sew all seams using mattress stitch (see Techniques: Sewing Up).

Join side seam of head and stuff. Join edges of each cheek to make a circle, then sew cheeks to face using photo as a guide for position. Join edges of each eye to make a circle, then sew each eye above a cheek. Using black embroidery thread (floss) and satin stitch (see Techniques: Satin Stitch), sew a pupil in each eye. Using Walnut, sew an outline around each eye using chain stitch (see Techniques: Chain Stitch). Sew side seam of nose and stuff. Secure to front of face. Embroider a curved smile in straight stitch (see Techniques: Straight Stitch) below nose using Walnut, then work back to fill gaps between stitches for a solid line. Fold ears in half, sew side seam and then secure each ear to top of head on either side.

Join side seam of body and stuff. Position head on cast-on edge of body and sew in place. Sew side seams of arms and each finger. Sew two fingers on either side of end on each arm. Sew an arm on each side of body **(E)**. Sew side seams of legs and shoes. Stuff shoes lightly, then gather cast-on edge to close. Secure a shoe to bottom of each leg. Sew legs to bottom of body. Sew side seam of tail, then sew to back of body.

Weave in all ends (see Techniques: Weaving in Ends).

Candy Cat

Candy Cat is one of Peppa's playgroup friends. She is quite independent and curious. She loves magic and fantasy stories. She enjoys skipping, dress-up, and is very good at playing tiger. Candy loves visiting the aquarium with her family and knows lots about fish.

Finished size

28cm (11in)

Needles

3.5mm (US size 4) straight needles

Other tools and materials

- Toy stuffing
- Small amount of black embroidery thread (floss)
- Tapestry needle

Yarn

Samples are made with Stylecraft Special DK (100% acrylic), DK (light worsted) weight, 295m (322yd) per 100g (3½oz) ball in the following shades:

- 35g Clementine (1853)
- 5g Fondant (1241)
- 10g White (1001)
- 10g Vintage Peach (1836)
- 10g Black (1002)
- 20g Kelly Green (1826)
- 5g Bright Pink (1435)

Aa
B
C

Head

Start from neck. Using Clementine, cast on 16 sts.

Row 1: [Kfb, k1] 8 times. (24 sts)

Row 2 and all even rows: P.

Row 3: [K1, kfb, k1] 8 times. (32 sts)

Row 5: [K2, kfb, k1] 8 times. (40 sts)

Row 7: [K3, kfb, k1] 8 times. (48 sts)

Row 9: [K4, kfb, k1] 8 times. (56 sts)

Row 11: [K5, kfb, k1] 8 times. (64 sts)

Rows 12–28: Starting with a p row, st st 17 rows.

Row 29: [K5, k2tog, k1] 8 times. (56 sts)

Row 31: [K4, k2tog, k1] 8 times. (48 sts)

Row 33: [K3, k2tog, k1] 8 times. (40 sts)

Row 35: [K2, k2tog, k1] 8 times. (32 sts)

Row 37: [K1, k2tog, k1] 8 times. (24 sts)

Row 39: [K2tog, k1] 8 times. (16 sts)

Row 41: [K2tog] 8 times. (8 sts)

Break yarn and thread through rem sts. Pull tight and fasten off.

Body

Start from neck. Using Clementine, cast on 24 sts.

Rows 1 and 2: Starting with a k row, st st 2 rows.

Row 3: [K1, kfb, k1] 8 times. (32 sts)

Row 4 and all even rows: P.

Row 5: [K2, kfb, k1] 8 times. (40 sts)

Row 7: [K3, kfb, k1] 8 times. (48 sts)

Row 9: [K4, kfb, k1] 8 times. (56 sts)

Rows 10–28: Starting with a p row, st st 19 rows.

Row 29: [K4, k2tog, k1] 8 times. (48 sts)

Row 31: [K3, k2tog, k1] 8 times. (40 sts)

Row 33: [K2, k2tog, k1] 8 times. (32 sts)

Row 35: [K1, k2tog, k1] 8 times. (24 sts)

Row 37: [K2tog, k1] 8 times. (16 sts)

Row 39: [K2tog] 8 times. (8 sts)

Break yarn and thread through rem sts. Pull tight and fasten off.

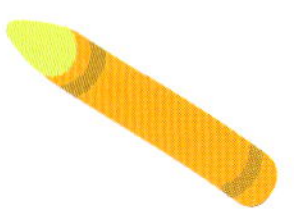

Arms

(make 2)

Using Clementine, cast on 5 sts.

Row 1: K.

Row 2: Cast on 2 sts, p to end. (7 sts)

Row 3: Cast on 2 sts, k to end. (9 sts)

Rows 4–24: Starting with a p row, st st 21 rows.

Row 25: K1, [k2tog] 4 times. (5 sts)

Break yarn and thread through rem sts. Pull tight and fasten off.

Fingers

(make 2 per arm)

Using Clementine, cast on 5 sts.

Row 1: K.

Row 2: Cast on 2 sts, p to end. (7 sts)

Row 3: Cast on 2 sts, k to end. (9 sts)

Rows 4–6: Starting with a p row, st st 3 rows.

Row 7: K1, [k2tog] 4 times. (5 sts)

Break yarn and thread through rem sts. Pull tight and fasten off.

Nose

Using Fondant, cast on 6 sts

Row 1 and all odd rows: P.

Row 2: K2tog, k2, k2tog. (4 sts)

Row 4: [K2tog] 2 times. (2 sts)

Break yarn and thread through rem sts. Pull tight and fasten off.

Ears

(make 2)

Using Clementine, cast on 20 sts.

Rows 1 and 2: Starting with a k row, st st 2 rows.

Row 3: [K1, k2tog, k4, k2tog, k1] 2 times. (16 sts)

Rows 4 and all even rows: P.

Row 5: [K1, k2tog, k2, k2tog, k1] 2 times. (12 sts)

Row 7: [K1, k2tog, k2tog, k1] 2 times. (8 sts)

Row 9: [K2tog] 4 times. (4 sts)

Row 10: [P2tog]2 times. (2 sts)

Break yarn and thread through rem sts. Pull tight and fasten off.

Tail

Using Clementine, cast on 10 sts.

Rows 1–22: Starting with a k row, st st 22 rows.

Row 23: [K2tog] 5 times. (5 sts)

Break yarn and thread through rem sts. Pull tight and fasten off **(A)**.

Eyes

(make 2)

Using White, cast on 14 sts.

Row 1: P.

Row 2: [K2tog] 7 times. (7 sts)

Break yarn and thread through rem sts. Pull tight and fasten off.

Cheeks

(make 2)

Using Vintage Peach, cast on 28 sts.

Row 1: P.

Row 2: [K2tog] 14 times. (14 sts)

Row 3: [P2tog] 7 times. (7 sts)

Break yarn and thread through rem sts. Pull tight and fasten off.

Legs

(make 2)

Using Clementine, cast on 10 sts.

Rows 1–19: Starting with a k row, st st 19 rows.

Cast (bind) off **(B)**.

Shoes

(make 2)

Using Black, cast on 6 sts.

Row 1: [Kfb] 6 times. (12 sts)

Rows 2–16: Starting with a p row, st st 13 rows.

Row 17: [K2tog] 6 times. (6 sts)

Break yarn and thread through rem sts. Pull tight and fasten off.

Dress

Start from bottom of dress. Using Kelly Green, cast on 72 sts.

Rows 1–4: G st 4 rows.

Rows 5–24: Starting with a k row, st st 20 rows.

Row 25: [K6, k2tog, k1] 8 times. (64 sts)

Row 26 and all even rows: P.

LEFT BACK

Work on first 16 sts only.

Row 27: [K5, k2tog, k1] 2 times. (14 sts)

Row 29: [K4, k2tog, k1] 2 times. (12 sts)

Row 31: [K3, k2tog, k1] 2 times. (10 sts)

Row 33: [K2, k2tog, k1] 2 times. (8 sts)

Break yarn.

FRONT

Rejoin yarn to centre 32 sts, work these 32 sts only.

Row 27: [K5, k2tog, k1] 4 times. (28 sts)

Row 29: [K4, k2tog, k1] 4 times. (24 sts)

Row 31: [K3, k2tog, k1] 4 times. (20 sts)

Row 33: [K2, k2tog, k1] 4 times. (16 sts)

Break yarn **(C)**.

RIGHT BACK

Rejoin yarn to last 16 sts and rep Rows 27–33 of left back.

Row 34: K8, join and k 16 sts for front, then join and k last 8 sts. (32 sts)

Cast (bind) off knitwise.

Assembly

Sew all seams using mattress stitch (see Techniques: Sewing Up).

Join side seam of head and stuff. Sew nose to centre of face **(E)**. Join edges of each cheek to make a circle, then sew cheeks to face using photo as a guide for position. Join edges of each eye to make a circle, then sew each eye above a cheek. Using black embroidery thread (floss) and satin stitch (see Techniques: Satin Stitch), sew a pupil in each eye. Using Vintage Peach, sew an outline around each eye using chain stitch (see Techniques: Chain Stitch). Embroider a curved smile in straight stitch (see Techniques: Straight Stitch) below nose using Bright Pink, then work back to fill gaps between stitches for a solid line. Embroider three straight lines either side of nose for whiskers using White **(E)**. Fold ears in half, sew side seam and then secure each ear to top of head on either side.

Join side seam of body and stuff. Position head on cast-on edge of body and sew in place. Place dress on body then sew side seam, leaving small gap for tail.

Sew side seams of arms and each finger. Sew two fingers on either side of end on each arm. Sew side seams of legs and shoes. Stuff shoes lightly, then gather cast-on edge to close. Secure a shoe to bottom of each leg. Sew legs to bottom of body. Sew side seam of tail. Using openings in dress as a guide, sew arms and tail **(D)** to body.

Weave in all ends (see Techniques: Weaving in Ends).

E

Difficulty

Gerald Giraffe

Gerald Giraffe is the tallest friend at playgroup. His dad is Mr. Giraffe, the zookeeper. Gerald is kind, wise, and caring. He is good at helping others and once rescued Dr. Hamster's tortoise, Tiddles, from a treetop. Gerald enjoys daydreaming and is very artistic. He also loves princesses and playing hide-and-seek – though hiding can be a challenge!

Finished size

32cm (12½in)

Needles

3.5mm (US size 4) straight needles

Other tools and materials

- Toy stuffing
- Small amount of black embroidery thread (floss)
- Tapestry needle

Yarn

Samples are made with Stylecraft Special DK (100% acrylic), DK (light worsted) weight, 295m (322yd) per 100g (3½oz) ball in the following shades:

- 35g Saffron (1081)
- 5g Blush (1833)
- 20g Lobelia (1825)
- 10g Powder Pink (1843)
- 10g White (1001)
- 10g Walnut (1054)
- 15g Gold (1709)
- 5g Copper (1029)
- 10g Black (1002)

Head

Start from neck. Using Saffron, cast on 16 sts.

Row 1: [Kfb, k1] 8 times. (24 sts)

Row 2 and all even rows: P.

Row 3: [K1, kfb, k1] 8 times. (32 sts)

Row 5: [K2, kfb, k1] 8 times. (40 sts)

Row 7: [K3, kfb, k1] 8 times. (48 sts)

Row 9: [K4, kfb, k1] 8 times. (56 sts)

Row 11: [K5, kfb, k1] 8 times. (64 sts)

Rows 12–34: Starting with a p row, st st 23 rows.

Row 35: [K5, k2tog, k1] 8 times. (56 sts)

Row 37: [K4, k2tog, k1] 8 times. (48 sts)

Row 39: [K3, k2tog, k1] 8 times. (40 sts)

Row 41: [K2, k2tog, k1] 8 times. (32 sts)

Break Saffron, join in Blush.

Rows 42–44: P 3 rows.

Row 45: K4, [k2tog] 4 times, k8, [k2tog] 4 times, k4. (24 sts)

Row 47: K2, [k2tog] 4 times, k4, [k2tog] 4 times, k2. (16 sts)

Row 49: [K2tog] 8 times. (8 sts)

Break yarn and thread through rem sts. Pull tight and fasten off **(A)**.

Body

Start from neck. Using Saffron, cast on 40 sts.

Rows 1–25: Starting with a k row, st st 25 rows.

Break Saffron, join in Lobelia.

Row 26: P.

Row 27: [K3, kfb, k1] 8 times. (48 sts)

Row 28 and all even rows: P.

Row 29: [K4, kfb, k1] 8 times. (56 sts)

Row 31: [K5, kfb, k1] 8 times. (64 sts)

Rows 32–52: Starting with a p row, st st 21 rows.

Row 53: [K5, k2tog, k1] 8 times. (56 sts)

Row 55: [K4, k2tog, k1] 8 times. (48 sts)

Row 57: [K3, k2tog, k1] 8 times. (40 sts)

Row 59: [K2, k2tog, k1] 8 times. (32 sts)

Row 61: [K1, k2tog, k1] 8 times. (24 sts)

Row 63: [K2tog, k1] 8 times. (16 sts)

Row 65: [K2tog] 8 times. (8 sts)

Break yarn and thread through rem sts. Pull tight and fasten off.

Arms

(make 2)

Using Saffron, cast on 5 sts.

Row 1: K.

Row 2: Cast on 2 sts, p to end. (7 sts)

Row 3: Cast on 2 sts, k to end. (9 sts)

Rows 4–24: Starting with a p row, st st 21 rows.

Row 25: K1, [k2tog] 4 times. (5 sts)

Break yarn and thread through rem sts. Pull tight and fasten off.

Fingers

(make 2 per arm)

Using Saffron, cast on 5 sts.

Row 1: K.

Row 2: Cast on 2 sts, p to end. (7 sts)

Row 3: Cast on 2 sts, k to end. (9 sts)

Rows 4–6: Starting with a p row, st st 3 rows.

Row 7: K1, [k2tog] 4 times. (5 sts)

Break yarn and thread through rem sts. Pull tight and fasten off.

Ears

(make 2)

Using Saffron, cast on 12 sts, then using Powder Pink cast on 12 sts.

Work all sts in colour presented on LH needle (pink sts in pink and yellow sts in yellow).

Rows 1 and 2: Starting with a k row, st st 2 rows.

Row 3: [K1, k2tog, k6, k2tog, k1] 2 times. (20 sts)

Rows 4 and all even rows: P.

Row 5: [K1, k2tog, k4, k2tog, k1] 2 times. (16 sts)

Row 7: [K1, k2tog, k2, k2tog, k1] 2 times. (12 sts)

Row 9: [K1, k2tog, k2tog, k1] 2 times. (8 sts)

Row 11: [K2tog] 4 times. (4 sts)

Break Powder Pink, continue in Saffron only.

Row 12: [P2tog] 2 times. (2 sts)

Break yarn and thread through rem sts. Pull tight and fasten off.

Tail

Using Saffron, cast on 10 sts.

Rows 1–16: Starting with a k row, st st 16 rows.

Break Saffron, join in Walnut.

Rows 17–22: Starting with a k row, st st 6 rows.

Row 23: [K2tog] 5 times. (5 sts)

Break yarn and thread through rem sts. Pull tight and fasten off **(B)**.

Tail ends

(make 2)

Using Walnut, cast on 5 sts.

Row 1: K.

Row 2: Cast on 2 sts, p to end. (7 sts)

Row 3: Cast on 2 sts, k to end. (9 sts)

Rows 4–6: Starting with a p row, st st 3 rows.

Row 7: K1, [k2tog] 4 times. (5 sts)

Break yarn and thread through rem sts. Pull tight and fasten off **(B)**.

A

B

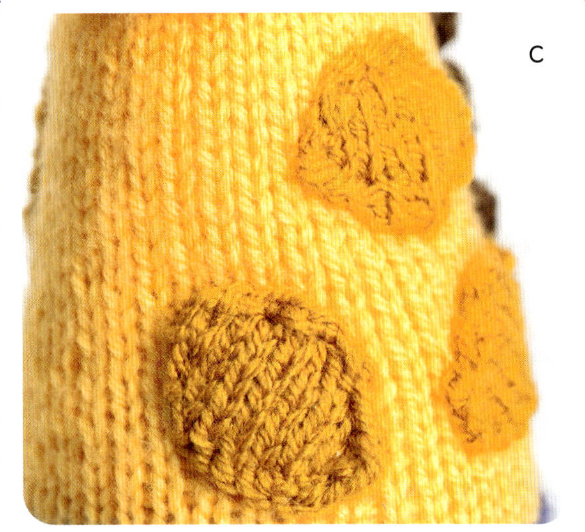

Eyes

(make 2)

Using White, cast on 14 sts.

Row 1: P.

Row 2: [K2tog] 7 times. (7 sts)

Break yarn and thread through rem sts. Pull tight and fasten off.

Spots

(make 10)

Using Gold, cast on 6 sts.

Row 1: Kfb, k4, kfb. (8 sts)

Row 2 and all even rows: P.

Row 3: Kfb, k6, kfb. (10 sts)

Row 5: Cast (bind) off 2 sts, then k to end. (8 sts)

Row 6: Cast (bind) off 2 sts, then p to end. (6 sts)

Row 7: [K2tog] 3 times. (3 sts)

Cast (bind) off **(C)**.

Legs

(make 2)

Using Saffron, cast on 10 sts.

Rows 1–19: Starting with a k row, st st 19 rows.

Cast (bind) off.

Shoes

(make 2)

Using Black, cast on 6 sts.

Row 1: [Kfb] 6 times. (12 sts)

Rows 2–16: Starting with a p row, st st 13 rows.

Row 17: [K2tog] 6 times. (6 sts)

Break yarn and thread through rem sts. Pull tight and fasten off.

Hair

(make 11)

Using Walnut, cast on 4 sts.

Rows 1–3: Starting with a k row, st st 3 rows.

Cast (bind) off **(D)**.

Assembly

Sew all seams using mattress stitch (see Techniques: Sewing Up).

Sew side seam of head and body and stuff. Join edges of each eye to make a circle, then sew each eye to face, using photo as a guide. Using black embroidery thread (floss) and satin stitch (see Techniques: Satin Stitch), sew a pupil in each eye. Using Gold, sew an outline around each eye using chain stitch (see Techniques: Chain Stitch). Fold cast-on edge of ears in half and sew side seam. Secure both ears to top of head and close cast-on edge of head. Using Black, embroider two nostrils in satin stitch **(E)**. Embroider a curved smile in straight stitch (see Techniques: Straight Stitch) below nose using Copper, then work back to fill gaps between stitches for a solid line **(E)**.

Position head on cast-on edge of body and sew in place.

Sew side seams of arms and each finger. Sew two fingers on either side of end on each arm, then sew an arm on each side of body using photos as a guide for position. Sew side seam of tail and tail parts. Sew two tail parts on either side of end on tail, then sew tail to back of body. Sew side seams of legs and shoes. Stuff shoes lightly, then gather cast-on edge to close. Secure a shoe to bottom of each leg. Sew legs to bottom of body. Sew three spots on either side of neck and two spots to either side of face. Sew hair pieces in a vertical line along back, using photos as reference.

Weave in all ends (see Techniques: Weaving in Ends).

Emily Elephant

Emily Elephant is a bit shy but loves to help others. She lives with her mum, Mrs. Elephant, her dad, Dr. Elephant, who is a dentist, and her brilliant little brother, Edmond. Emily is very good at building blocks, and she can make loud noises with her trunk. Her favourite game is the same as Peppa's: jumping up and down in muddy puddles.

Finished size

27cm (10½in) tall sitting, to tip of ears

Needles

3.5mm (US size 4) straight needles

Other tools and materials

- Toy stuffing
- Small amount of black embroidery thread (floss)
- Tapestry needle

Yarn

Samples are made with Stylecraft Special DK (100% acrylic), DK (light worsted) weight, 295m (322yd) per 100g (3½oz) ball in the following shades:

- 35g Parma Violet (1724)
- 10g White (1001)
- 10g Clematis (1390)
- 10g Black (1002)
- 20g Dandelion (1856)
- 5g Lavender (1188)
- 5g Raspberry (1023)

Head

Start from back. Using Parma Violet, cast on 16 sts.

Row 1: [Kfb, k1] 8 times. (24 sts)

Row 2 and all even rows: P.

Row 3: [K1, kfb, k1] 8 times. (32 sts)

Row 5: [K2, kfb, k1] 8 times. (40 sts)

Row 7: [K3, kfb, k1] 8 times. (48 sts)

Row 9: [K4, kfb, k1] 8 times. (56 sts)

Row 11: [K5, kfb, k1] 8 times. (64 sts)

Rows 12–28: Starting with a p row, st st 17 rows.

Row 29: [K5, k2tog, k1] 8 times. (56 sts)

Row 31: K1, ssk, k to last 3 sts, k2tog, k1. (54 sts)

Row 32: P.

Rows 33–38: Rep Rows 31 and 32. (48 sts)

Row 39: Cast (bind) off 2 sts, k to end. (46 sts)

Row 40: Cast (bind) off 2 sts, p to end. (44 sts)

Row 41: Cast (bind) off 2 sts, k to end. (42 sts)

Row 42: Cast (bind) off 2 sts, p to end. (40 sts)

Rows 43 and 44: Starting with a k row, st st 2 rows.

Row 45: [K2, k2tog, k1] 8 times. (32 sts)

Rows 46–48: Starting with a p row, st st 3 rows.

Row 49: [K1, k2tog, k1] 8 times. (24 sts)

Rows 50–54: Starting with a p row, st st 5 rows.

Row 55: K2tog, k20, k2tog. (22 sts)

Rows 56–60: Starting with a p row, st st 5 rows.

Row 61: K2tog, k18, k2tog. (20 sts)

Rows 62–66: Starting with a p row, st st 5 rows.

Row 67: K2tog, k16, k2tog. (18 sts)

Rows 68–72: Starting with a p row, st st 5 rows.

Row 73: K2tog, k14, k2tog. (16 sts)

Rows 74–78: Starting with a p row, st st 5 rows.

Row 79: [K2tog] 8 times. (8 sts)

Break yarn and thread through rem sts. Pull tight and fasten off **(A)**.

Body

Start from neck. Using Parma Violet, cast on 24 sts.

Rows 1 and 2: Starting with a k row, st st 2 rows.

Row 3: [K1, kfb, k1] 8 times. (32 sts)

Row 4 and all even rows: P.

Row 5: [K2, kfb, k1] 8 times. (40 sts)

Row 7: [K3, kfb, k1] 8 times. (48 sts)

Row 9: [K4, kfb, k1] 8 times. (56 sts)

Rows 10–28: Starting with a p row, st st 19 rows.

Row 29: [K4, k2tog, k1] 8 times. (48 sts)

Row 31: [K3, k2tog, k1] 8 times. (40 sts)

Row 33: [K2, k2tog, k1] 8 times. (32 sts)

Row 35: [K1, k2tog, k1] 8 times. (24 sts)

Row 37: [K2tog, k1] 8 times. (16 sts)

Row 39: [K2tog] 8 times. (8 sts)

Break yarn and thread through rem sts. Pull tight and fasten off **(B)**.

Arms

(make 2)

Using Parma Violet, cast on 5 sts.

Row 1: K.

Row 2: Cast on 2 sts, p to end. (7 sts)

Row 3: Cast on 2 sts, k to end. (9 sts)

Rows 4–24: Starting with a p row, st st 21 rows.

Row 25: K1, [k2tog] 4 times. (5 sts)

Break yarn and thread through rem sts. Pull tight and fasten off.

Fingers

(make 2 per arm)

Using Parma Violet, cast on 5 sts.

Row 1: K.

Row 2: Cast on 2 sts, p to end. (7 sts)

Row 3: Cast on 2 sts, k to end. (9 sts)

Rows 4–6: Starting with a p row, st st 3 rows.

Row 7: K1, [k2tog] 4 times. (5 sts)

Break yarn and thread through rem sts. Pull tight and fasten off.

Ears

(make 2)

Using Parma Violet, cast on 24 sts.

Row 1: [K1, kfb, k8, kfb, k1] 2 times. (28 sts)

Row 2 and all even rows: P.

Row 3: [K1, kfb, k10, kfb, k1] 2 times. (32 sts)

Row 5: [K1, kfb, k12, kfb, k1] 2 times. (36 sts)

Rows 6–12: Starting with a p row, st st 7 rows.

Row 13: [K1, k2tog, k12, k2tog, k1] 2 times. (32 sts)

Row 15: [K1, k2tog, k10, k2tog, k1] 2 times. (28 sts)

Row 17: [K1, k2tog, k8, k2tog, k1] 2 times. (24 sts)

Row 19: [K1, k2tog, k6, k2tog, k1] 2 times. (20 sts)

Row 21: [K1, k2tog, k4, k2tog, k1] 2 times. (16 sts)

Row 23: [K2tog] 8 times. (8 sts)

Break yarn and thread through rem sts. Pull tight and fasten off **(C)**.

C

Tail

Using Parma Violet, cast on 10 sts.

Rows 1–22: Starting with a k row, st st 22 rows.

Row 23: [K2tog] 5 times. (5 sts)

Break yarn and thread through rem sts. Pull tight and fasten off.

Tail ends

(make 2)

Using Parma Violet, cast on 5 sts.

Row 1: K.

Row 2: Cast on 2 sts, p to end. (7 sts)

Row 3: Cast on 2 sts, k to end. (9 sts)

Rows 4–6: Starting with a p row, st st 3 rows.

Row 7: K1, [k2tog] 4 times. (5 sts)

Break yarn and thread through rem sts. Pull tight and fasten off.

Eyes

(make 2)

Using White, cast on 14 sts.

Row 1: P.

Row 2: [K2tog] 7 times. (7 sts)

Break yarn and thread through rem sts. Pull tight and fasten off.

Cheeks

(make 2)

Using Clematis, cast on 28 sts.

Row 1: P.

Row 2: [K2tog] 14 times. (14 sts)

Row 3: [P2tog] 7 times. (7 sts)

Break yarn and thread through rem sts. Pull tight and fasten off.

Legs

(make 2)

Using Parma Violet, cast on 10 sts.

Rows 1–19: Starting with a k row, st st 19 rows.

Cast (bind) off.

Shoes

(make 2)

Using Black, cast on 6 sts.

Row 1: [Kfb] 6 times. (12 sts)

Rows 2–14: Starting with a p row, st st 13 rows.

Row 15: [K2tog] 6 times. (6 sts)

Break yarn and thread through rem sts. Pull tight and fasten off.

Dress

Start from bottom. Using Dandelion, cast on 72 sts.

Rows 1–4: G st 4 rows.

Rows 5–24: Starting with a k row, st st 20 rows.

Row 25: [K6, k2tog, k1] 8 times. (64 sts)

Row 26 and all even rows: P.

LEFT BACK

Work on first 16 sts only.

Row 27: [K5, k2tog, k1] 2 times. (14 sts)

Row 29: [K4, k2tog, k1] 2 times. (12 sts)

Row 31: [K3, k2tog, k1] 2 times. (10 sts)

Row 33: [K2, k2tog, k1] 2 times. (8 sts)

Break yarn.

FRONT

Rejoin yarn to centre 32 sts, work these 32 sts only.

Row 27: [K5, k2tog, k1] 4 times. (28 sts)

Row 29: [K4, k2tog, k1] 4 times. (24 sts)

Row 31: [K3, k2tog, k1] 4 times. (20 sts)

Row 33: [K2, k2tog, k1] 4 times. (16 sts)

Break yarn.

RIGHT BACK

Rejoin yarn to last 16 sts and rep Rows 27–33 of left back.

Row 34: K8, join and k 16 sts for front, then join and k last 8 sts. (32 sts)

Cast (bind) off knitwise.

Assembly

Sew all seams using mattress stitch (see Techniques: Sewing Up).

Join side seam of head and stuff. Join edges of each cheek to make a circle, then sew cheeks to face using photo as a guide for position. Join edges of each eye to make a circle, then sew each eye above a cheek. Using black embroidery thread (floss) and satin stitch (see Techniques: Satin Stitch), sew a pupil in each eye.

Using Lavender, sew an outline around each eye using chain stitch (see Techniques: Chain Stitch) **(D)** and four straight lines across trunk for wrinkles **(E)**. Embroider a curved smile in straight stitch (see Techniques: Straight Stitch) using Raspberry, then work back to fill gaps between stitches for a solid line. Fold ears in half, sew side seam and then secure each ear to top of head on either side.

Join side seam of body and stuff. Position head on cast-on edge of body and sew in place. Place dress on body then sew side seam, leaving small gap for tail.

Sew side seams of arms and each finger. Sew two fingers on either side of end on each arm. Sew side seam of tail and each tail end. Sew tail end on either side of end of tail. Sew side seams of legs and shoes. Stuff shoes lightly, then gather cast-on edge to close. Secure a shoe to bottom of each leg. Sew legs to bottom of body. Using openings in dress as a guide, sew arms and tail to body.

Weave in all ends (see Techniques: Weaving in Ends).

Difficulty

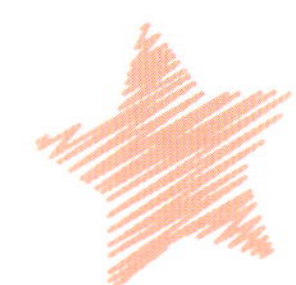

Freddy Fox

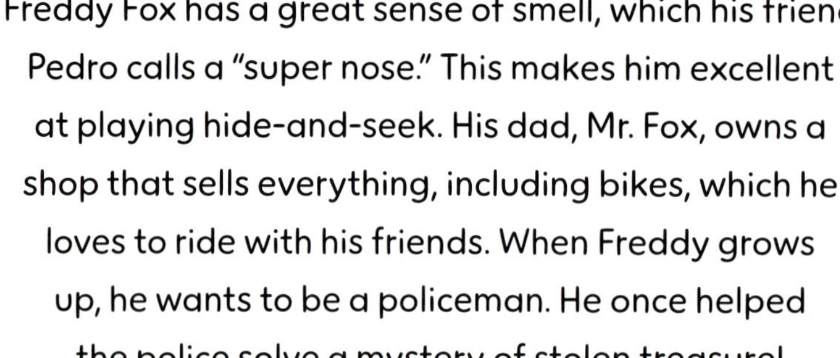

Freddy Fox has a great sense of smell, which his friend Pedro calls a "super nose." This makes him excellent at playing hide-and-seek. His dad, Mr. Fox, owns a shop that sells everything, including bikes, which he loves to ride with his friends. When Freddy grows up, he wants to be a policeman. He once helped the police solve a mystery of stolen treasure!

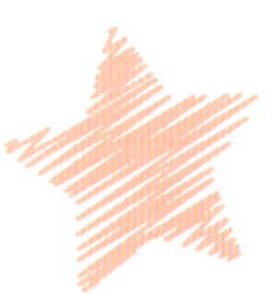

Finished size

26cm (10¼in)

Needles

3.5mm (US size 4) straight needles

Other tools and materials

- Toy stuffing
- Small amount of black embroidery thread (floss)
- Tapestry needle

Yarn

Samples are made with Stylecraft Special DK (100% acrylic), DK (light worsted) weight, 295m (322yd) per 100g (3½oz) ball in the following shades:

- 35g Spice (1711)
- 20g Copper (1029)
- 10g White (1001)
- 10g Shrimp (1132)
- 10g Black (1002)
- 5g Gingerbread (1806)
- 5g Raspberry (1023)

5
6
8
9
A

Head

Start from neck. Using Spice, cast on 16 sts.

Row 1: [Kfb, k1] 8 times. (24 sts)

Row 2 and all even rows: P.

Row 3: [K1, kfb, k1] 8 times. (32 sts)

Row 5: [K2, kfb, k1] 8 times. (40 sts)

Row 7: [K3, kfb, k1] 8 times. (48 sts)

Row 9: [K4, kfb, k1] 8 times. (56 sts)

Row 11: [K5, kfb, k1] 8 times. (64 sts)

Rows 12–34: Starting with a p row, st st 23 rows.

Row 35: [K5, k2tog, k1] 8 times. (56 sts)

Row 37: [K4, k2tog, k1] 8 times. (48 sts)

Row 39: [K3, k2tog, k1] 8 times. (40 sts)

Row 41: [K2, k2tog, k1] 8 times. (32 sts)

Break Spice, join in Black.

Row 42: P.

Row 43: [K1, k2tog, k1] 8 times. (24 sts)

Rows 44–46: Starting with a p row, st st 3 rows.

Row 47: [K2tog, k1] 8 times. (16 sts)

Rows 48–50: Starting with a p row, st st 3 rows.

Row 51: [K2tog] 8 times. (8 sts)

Rows 52–54: Starting with a p row, st st 3 rows.

Row 55: [K2tog] 4 times. (4 sts)

Break yarn and thread through rem sts. Pull tight and fasten off **(A)**.

Body

Start from neck. Using Copper, cast on 24 sts.

Rows 1 and 2: Starting with a k row, st st 2 rows.

Row 3: [K1, kfb, k1] 8 times. (32 sts)

Row 4 and all even rows: P.

Row 5: [K2, kfb, k1] 8 times. (40 sts)

Row 7: [K3, kfb, k1] 8 times. (48 sts)

Row 9: [K4, kfb, k1] 8 times. (56 sts)

Rows 10–28: Starting with a p row, st st 19 rows.

Row 29: [K4, k2tog, k1] 8 times. (48 sts)

Row 31: [K3, k2tog, k1] 8 times. (40 sts)

Row 33: [K2, k2tog, k1] 8 times. (32 sts)

Row 35: [K1, k2tog, k1] 8 times. (24 sts)

Row 37: [K2tog, k1] 8 times. (16 sts)

Row 39: [K2tog] 8 times. (8 sts)

Break yarn and thread through rem sts. Pull tight and fasten off.

Arms

(make 2)

Using Spice, cast on 5 sts.

Row 1: K.

Row 2: Cast on 2 sts, p to end. (7 sts)

Row 3: Cast on 2 sts, k to end. (9 sts)

Rows 4–24: Starting with a p row, st st 21 rows.

Row 25: K1, [k2tog] 4 times. (5 sts)

Break yarn and thread through rem sts. Pull tight and fasten off.

Fingers

(make 2 per arm)

Using Spice, cast on 5 sts.

Row 1: K.

Row 2: Cast on 2 sts, p to end. (7 sts)

Row 3: Cast on 2 sts, k to end. (9 sts)

Rows 4–6: Starting with a p row, st st 3 rows.

Row 7: K1, [k2tog] 4 times. (5 sts)

Break yarn and thread through rem sts. Pull tight and fasten off.

Ears

(make 2)

Using Spice, cast on 24 sts.

Rows 1 and 2: Starting with a k row, st st 2 rows.

Row 3: [K1, k2tog, k6, k2tog, k1] 2 times. (20 sts)

Row 4 and all even rows: P.

Row 5: [K1, k2tog, k4, k2tog, k1] 2 times. (16 sts)

Row 7: [K1, k2tog, k2, k2tog, k1] 2 times. (12 sts)

Row 9: [K1, k2tog, k2tog, k1] 2 times. (8 sts)

Row 11: [K2tog] 4 times. (4 sts)

Row 12: [P2tog] 2 times. (2 sts)

Break yarn and thread through rem sts. Pull tight and fasten off.

Tail

Using Spice, cast on 16 sts.

Rows 1 and 2: Starting with a k row, st st 2 rows.

Row 3: [K2, kfb, k1] 4 times. (20 sts)

Rows 4–6: Starting with a p row, st st 3 rows.

Row 7: [K3, kfb, k1] 4 times. (24 sts)

Rows 8–14: Starting with a p row, st st 7 rows.

Row 15: K17, w&t, p10, w&t, k8, w&t, p6, w&t, k4, w&t, p2, w&t, k to end.

Rows 16–22: Starting with a p row, st st 7 rows.

Break Spice, join in White.

Row 23: K.

Row 24 and all even rows: P.

Row 25: [K3, k2tog, k1] 4 times. (20 sts)

Row 27: [K2, k2tog, k1] 4 times. (16 sts)

Row 29: [K1, k2tog, k1] 4 times. (12 sts)

Row 31: [K2tog, k1] 4 times. (8 sts)

Row 33: [K2tog] 4 times. (4 sts)

Break yarn and thread through rem sts. Pull tight and fasten off **(B)**.

Eyes

(make 2)

Using White, cast on 14 sts.

Row 1: P.

Row 2: [K2tog] 7 times. (7 sts)

Break yarn and thread through rem sts. Pull tight and fasten off.

Cheeks

(make 2)

Using Shrimp, cast on 28 sts.

Row 1: P.

Row 2: [K2tog] 14 times. (14 sts)

Row 3: [P2tog] 7 times. (7 sts)

Break yarn and thread through rem sts. Pull tight and fasten off **(C)**.

Legs

(make 2)

Using Spice, cast on 10 sts.

Rows 1–19: Starting with a k row, st st 19 rows.

Cast (bind) off.

Shoes

(make 2)

Using Black, cast on 6 sts.

Row 1: [Kfb] 6 times. (12 sts)

Rows 2–14: Starting with a p row, st st 13 rows.

Row 15: [K2tog] 6 times. (6 sts)

Break yarn and thread through rem sts. Pull tight and fasten off.

Assembly

Sew all seams using mattress stitch (see Techniques: Sewing Up).

Join side seam of head and stuff. Join edges of each cheek to make a circle, then sew cheeks to face using photo as a guide for position. Join edges of each eye to make a circle, then sew each eye above a cheek. Using black embroidery thread (floss) and satin stitch (see Techniques: Satin Stitch), sew a pupil in each eye. Using Gingerbread, sew an outline around each eye using chain stitch (see Techniques: Chain Stitch) **(D)**. Embroider a curved smile in straight stitch (see Techniques: Straight Stitch) using Raspberry, then work back to fill gaps between stitches for a solid line. Fold ears in half, sew along side seam and then secure each ear to top of head on either side **(E)**.

Join side seam of body and stuff. Position head on cast-on edge of body and sew in place. Sew side seams of arms and each finger. Sew two fingers on either side of end on each arm, then sew arms to either side of body. Sew side seams of legs and shoes. Stuff shoes lightly, then gather cast-on edge to close. Secure a shoe to bottom of each leg. Sew legs to bottom of body. Sew side seam of tail and stuff, then sew to back of body.

Weave in all ends (see Techniques: Weaving in Ends).

E

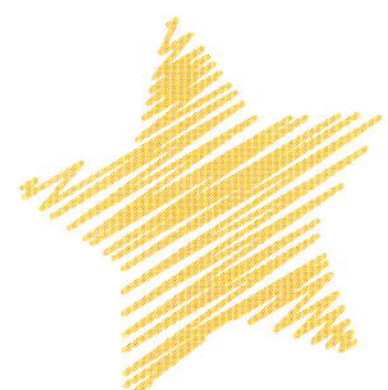

Difficulty

Zoë Zebra

Zoë Zebra enjoys all things musical, especially singing. She adores her toy monkey, having picnics and tea parties. Her mummy even helped her make a clay tea set. Her dad, Mr. Zebra, is the postman, and she likes to help him deliver letters and parcels. She is also a wise older sister to two twin sisters, Zuzu and Zaza.

Finished size

25cm (9¾in)

Needles

3.5mm (US size 4) straight needles

Other tools and materials

- Toy stuffing
- Small amount of black embroidery thread (floss)
- Tapestry needle

Yarn

Samples are made with Stylecraft Special DK (100% acrylic), DK (light worsted) weight, 295m (322yd) per 100g (3½oz) ball in the following shades:

- 25g Black (1002)
- 20g White (1001)
- 5g Fondant (1241)
- 20g Fuchsia Purple (1827)
- 5g Grey (1099)
- 5g Bright Pink (1435)
- 5g Raspberry (1023)

Head

Start from neck. Using Black, cast on 16 sts.

Row 1: [Kfb, k1] 8 times. (24 sts)

Row 2 and all even rows: P.

Row 3: [K1, kfb, k1] 8 times. (32 sts)

Row 5: [K2, kfb, k1] 8 times. (40 sts)

Row 7: [K3, kfb, k1] 8 times. (48 sts)

Row 9: [K4, kfb, k1] 8 times. (56 sts)

Row 10: Change to White, p to end.

Row 11: [K5, kfb, k1] 8 times. (64 sts)

Rows 12–19: Starting with a p row, st st 8 rows.

Row 20: Change to Black, p to end.

Rows 21–29: Starting with a k row, st st 9 rows.

Row 30: Change to White, p to end.

Rows 31–34: Starting with a k row, st st 4 rows.

Row 35: [K5, k2tog, k1] 8 times. (56 sts)

Row 37: [K4, k2tog, k1] 8 times. (48 sts)

Row 39: [K3, k2tog, k1] 8 times. (40 sts)

Row 41: [K2, k2tog, k1] 8 times. (32 sts)

Rows 42–44: Change to Fondant, p 3 rows.

Row 45: K4, [k2tog] 4 times, k8, [k2tog] 4 times, k4. (24 sts)

Row 47: K2, [k2tog] 4 times, k4, [k2tog] 4 times, k2. (16 sts)

Row 49: [K2tog] 8 times. (8 sts)

Break yarn and thread through rem sts. Pull tight and fasten off **(A)**.

Body

Start from neck. Using Black, cast on 24 sts.

Rows 1 and 2: Starting with a k row, st st 2 rows.

Row 3: [K1, kfb, k1] 8 times. (32 sts)

Row 4 and all even rows: P.

Row 5: [K2, kfb, k1] 8 times. (40 sts)

Row 7: [K3, kfb, k1] 8 times. (48 sts)

Row 9: [K4, kfb, k1] 8 times. (56 sts)

Rows 10–19: Change to White, starting with a p row, st st 10 rows.

Rows 20–28: Change to Black, starting with a p row, st st 9 rows

Row 29: [K4, k2tog, k1] 8 times. (48 sts)

Row 30: Change to White, p to end.

Row 31: [K3, k2tog, k1] 8 times. (40 sts)

Row 33: [K2, k2tog, k1] 8 times. (32 sts)

Row 35: [K1, k2tog, k1] 8 times. (24 sts)

Row 37: [K2tog, k1] 8 times. (16 sts)

Row 39: [K2tog] 8 times. (8 sts)

Break yarn and thread through rem sts. Pull tight and fasten off **(B)**.

Arms

(make 2)

Using White, cast on 5 sts.

Row 1: K.

Row 2: Cast on 2 sts, p to end. (7 sts)

Row 3: Cast on 2 sts, k to end. (9 sts)

Rows 4–6: Starting with a p row, st st 3 rows.

Rows 7–12: Change to Black, starting with a p row, st st 6 rows.

Rows 13–18: Change to White, starting with a p row, st st 6 rows.

Rows 19–24: Change to Black, starting with a p row, st st 6 rows.

Row 25: K1, [k2tog] 4 times. (5 sts)

Break yarn and thread through rem sts. Pull tight and fasten off **(B)**.

Fingers

(make 2 per arm)

Using Black, cast on 5 sts.

Row 1: K.

Row 2: Cast on 2 sts, p to end. (7 sts)

Row 3: Cast on 2 sts, k to end. (9 sts)

Rows 4–6: Starting with a p row, st st 3 rows.

Row 7: K1, [k2tog] 4 times. (5 sts)

Break yarn and thread through rem sts. Pull tight and fasten off.

Ears

(make 1 in Black, 1 in White)

Cast on 18 sts using Black or White.

Rows 1–6: Starting with a k row, st st 6 rows.

Row 7: [K2tog, k1] 6 times. (12 sts)

Row 8: P.

Row 9: [K2tog] 6 times. (6 sts)

Break yarn and thread through rem sts. Pull tight and fasten off.

Tail

Using Black, cast on 10 sts.

Rows 1–22: Starting with a k row, st st 22 rows.

Row 23: [K2tog] 5 times. (5 sts)

Break yarn and thread through rem sts. Pull tight and fasten off.

Tail ends

(make 2)

Using Black, cast on 5 sts.

Row 1: K.

Row 2: Cast on 2 sts, p to end. (7 sts)

Row 3: Cast on 2 sts, k to end. (9 sts)

Rows 4–6: Starting with a p row, st st 3 rows.

Row 7: K1, [k2tog] 4 times. (5 sts)

Break yarn and thread through rem sts. Pull tight and fasten off.

A

B

Eyes

(make 2)

Using White, cast on 14 sts.

Row 1: P.

Row 2: [K2tog] 7 times. (7 sts)

Break yarn and thread through rem sts. Pull tight and fasten off.

Legs

(make 2)

Using Black, cast on 10 sts.

Rows 1–5: Starting with a k row, st st 5 rows.

Rows 6–10: Change to White, starting with a p row, st st 5 rows.

Rows 11–15: Change to Black, starting with a k row, st st 5 rows

Rows 16–19: Change to White, starting with a p row, st st 4 rows.

Cast (bind) off **(C)**.

Shoes

(make 2)

Using Black, cast on 6 sts.

Row 1: [Kfb] 6 times. (12 sts)

Rows 2–14: Starting with a p row, st st 13 rows.

Row 15: [K2tog] 6 times. (6 sts)

Break yarn and thread through rem sts. Pull tight and fasten off **(C)**.

Dress

Start from bottom of dress. Using Fuchsia Purple, cast on 72 sts.

Rows 1–4: G st 4 rows.

Rows 5–24: Starting with a k row, st st 20 rows.

Row 25: [K6, k2tog, k1] 8 times. (64 sts)

Row 26 and all even rows: P.

LEFT BACK

Work on first 16 sts only.

Row 27: [K5, k2tog, k1] 2 times. (14 sts)

Row 29: [K4, k2tog, k1] 2 times. (12 sts)

Row 31: [K3, k2tog, k1] 2 times. (10 sts)

Row 33: [K2, k2tog, k1] 2 times. (8 sts)

Break yarn.

FRONT

Rejoin yarn to centre 32 sts, work these 32 sts only.

Row 27: [K5, k2tog, k1] 4 times. (8 sts)

Row 29: [K4, k2tog, k1] 4 times. (24 sts)

Row 31: [K3, k2tog, k1] 4 times. (20 sts)

Row 33: [K2, k2tog, k1] 4 times. (16 sts)

Break yarn.

RIGHT BACK

Rejoin yarn to last 16 sts and rep Rows 27–33 of left back.

Row 34: K8, join and k 16 sts for front, then join and k last 8 sts. (32 sts)

Cast (bind) off knitwise.

Assembly

Sew all seams using mattress stitch (see Techniques: Sewing Up).

Join side seam of head and stuff. Join edges of each eye to make a circle, then sew each eye above a cheek, using photo as a guide. Using black embroidery thread (floss) and satin stitch (see Techniques: Satin Stitch), sew a pupil in each eye. Using Grey, sew an outline around each eye using chain stitch (see Techniques: Chain Stitch). Embroider a curved smile in straight stitch (see Techniques: Straight Stitch) using Bright Pink, then work back to fill gaps between stitches for a solid line. Embroider nostrils in Raspberry **(D)**. Fold cast-on edge of ears in half, sew side seam and then secure each ear to top of head on either side.

Join side seam of body and stuff. Position head on cast-on edge of body and sew in place. Place dress on body then sew side seam, leaving small gap for tail. Sew side seams of arms and each finger. Sew two fingers on either side of end on each arm **(E)**. Sew side seam of tail and each tail end. Sew tail end on either side of end of tail. Sew side seams of legs and shoes. Stuff shoes lightly, then gather cast-on edge to close. Secure a shoe to bottom of each leg. Sew legs to bottom of body. Using openings in dress as a guide, sew arms and tail to body.

Weave in all ends (see Techniques: Weaving in Ends).

D

E

Techniques

Here are all the stitches and other techniques that you will need for the projects in this book.

Cable cast on

There are many different ways of casting on yarn; for knitting toys, I find the cable cast on gives a neat and even edge. Start by making a slip knot on the left-hand needle **(A)**. To make the second stitch, place the right-hand needle into the slip knot and loop the yarn around it **(B)**. Pull the loop through to make a stitch on the right-hand needle **(C)**, then transfer the stitch to the left-hand needle. For all following stitches, place the right-hand needle between the last two stitches on the left-hand needle and loop the yarn around the tip **(D)**. Pull the loop over and onto the left-hand needle. Repeat until you have the number of stitches you need.

Knit stitch

Starting with stitches on the left-hand needle and the yarn behind the work, insert the tip of the right-hand needle into the front of the first stitch **(E)**. Wrap the yarn around your right-hand needle clockwise **(F)** and pull the loop through the first stitch **(G)**, sliding the worked stitch off the left-hand needle and on to the right-hand one **(H)**. Repeat this until all the stitches are on the right-hand needle. Swap the needles over and repeat. For a clean edge, slide the first stitch onto the right-hand needle without knitting it, then knit all the stitches to the end of the row.

Purl stitch

This time start with the yarn in front, bring the tip of the right-hand needle through the front of the first stitch **(I)**. Wrap the yarn counter clockwise around the tip of the needle **(J)** and pull the loop through the back of the stitch **(K)**. Slide the worked stitch off the left-hand needle **(L)** and repeat. As with the knitted stitches, slide the first stitch onto the right-hand needle without purling it for a sharp edge.

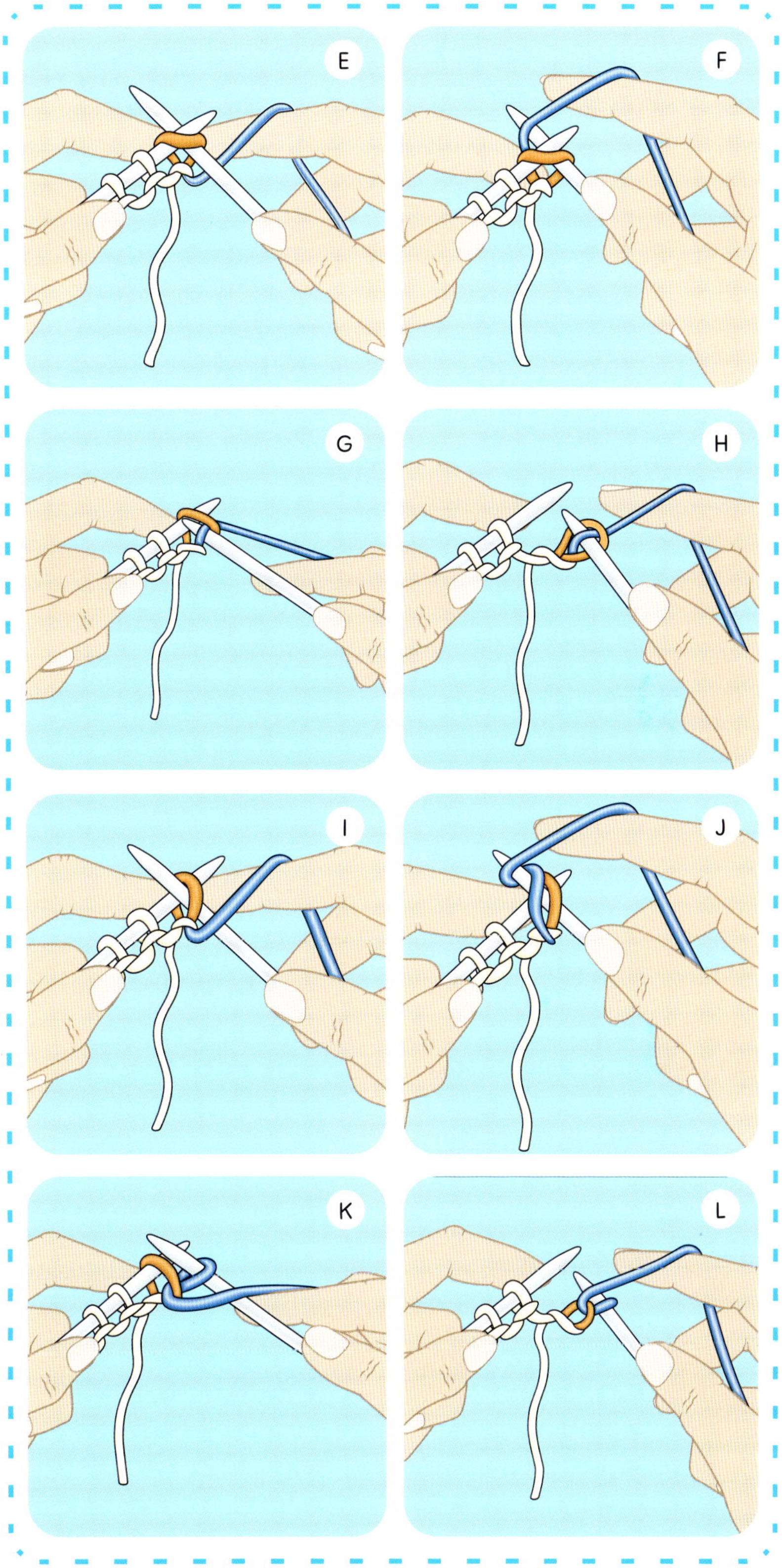

Cast (bind) off

At the end of the piece you must cast (bind) the knitting off the needles. To do this, knit (or purl if on the purl side) the first two stitches, then insert the left-hand needle into the first stitch on the right-hand needle **(A)** and pull this stitch up and over the second stitch **(B)** you just worked to cast (bind) off the first stitch **(C)**. Repeat this process until one stitch remains. Cut the yarn, draw the yarn end through the last stitch and fasten tightly.

Joining a new colour

To change to a new colour, insert the right-hand needle into the first stitch on the left-hand needle and wrap both old and new colours around the needle **(D).** Purl (or knit) the first stitch with both colours **(E)**. For the next couple of stitches, only use the new colour by wrapping the yarn and the tail end around the needle to work the stitch to ensure the yarn is secured. Carry on in the new colour. When you reach the double stitch in both colours, work both strands as one stitch **(F)**.

Weaving in ends

Once you've blocked your piece it's time to get rid of those loose yarn ends. Thread a tapestry needle with each strand and, one at a time, thread them through four or five stitches on the back of the work **(G)** and then cut off the left-over yarn.

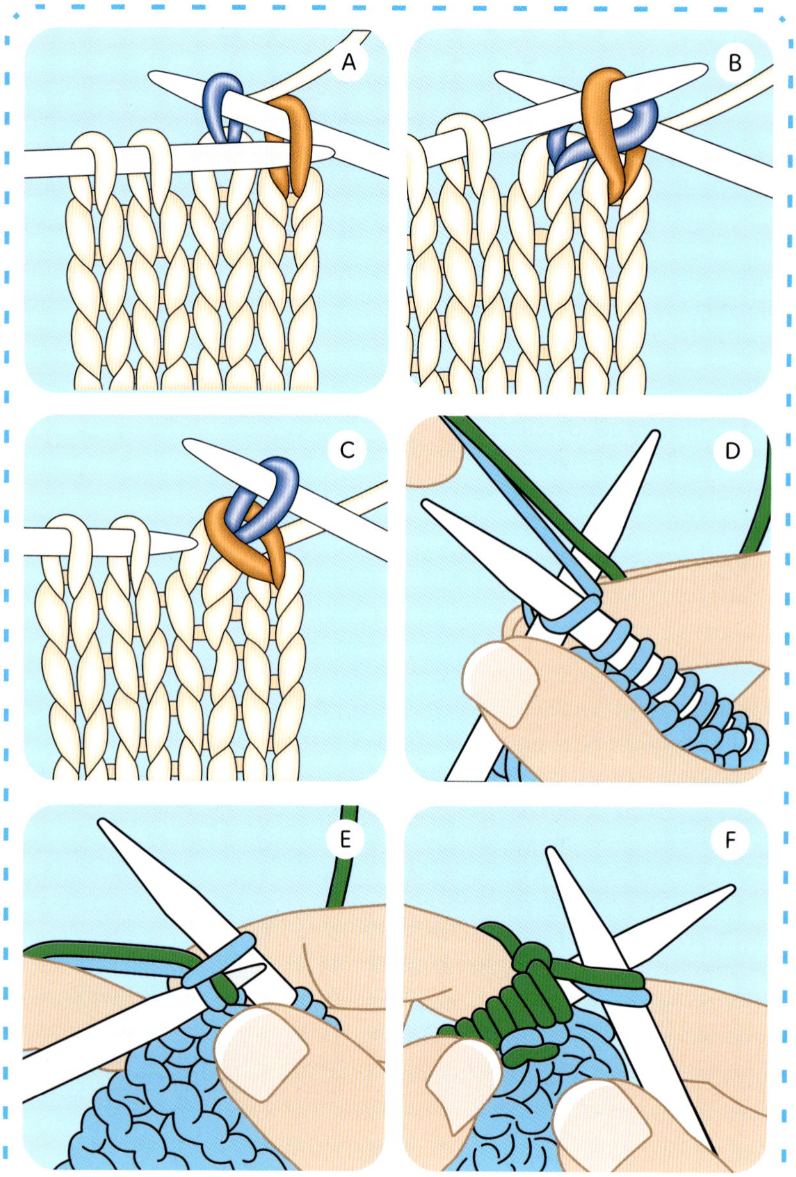

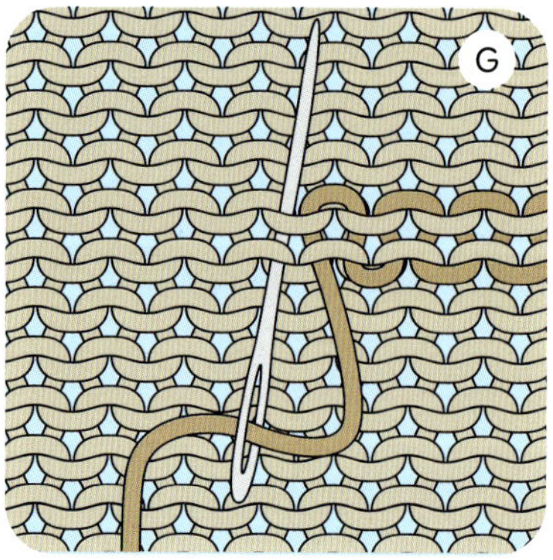

Short rows

A short row is only part worked to create shaping. Work to the turning point and slip the next stitch from the left-hand needle to the right-hand needle. Bring the yarn to the front **(H)** and slip the same stitch back to the left-hand needle. Bring the yarn back to the back to 'wrap' the stitch **(I)**. Turn and purl to the turning point, take the yarn back and slip the next stitch to the right-hand needle **(J)**. Bring the yarn to the front, move the slipped needle back to the left-hand needle **(K)**.

To stop the horizontal bar showing when working wrapped stitches, insert the tip of your right-hand needle into the wrap and next working stitch and knit them together. On a purl row, pick up the wrap from the back on the left-hand needle, then purl the wrap and the stitch together.

Yarn over eyelet

Yarn overs make a small hole in the fabric, ideal for tiny buttonholes. Knit the desired stitches, then bring the yarn to the front and wrap it over the right-hand needle before working the next stitch **(L)**. The yarn over is worked as a normal stitch in the next row.

Making a tiny pompom

Start by wrapping the yarn around a fork, leaving space at the bottom and the top. Wrap about 20–30 times **(M)**. Cut the yarn and thread another piece of yarn through the bottom of the fork from front to back. Pull the ends upwards and tie securely in a knot. Carefully slide the wraps from the fork **(N)** and snip the loops **(O)**. Trim the pompom if necessary to neaten.

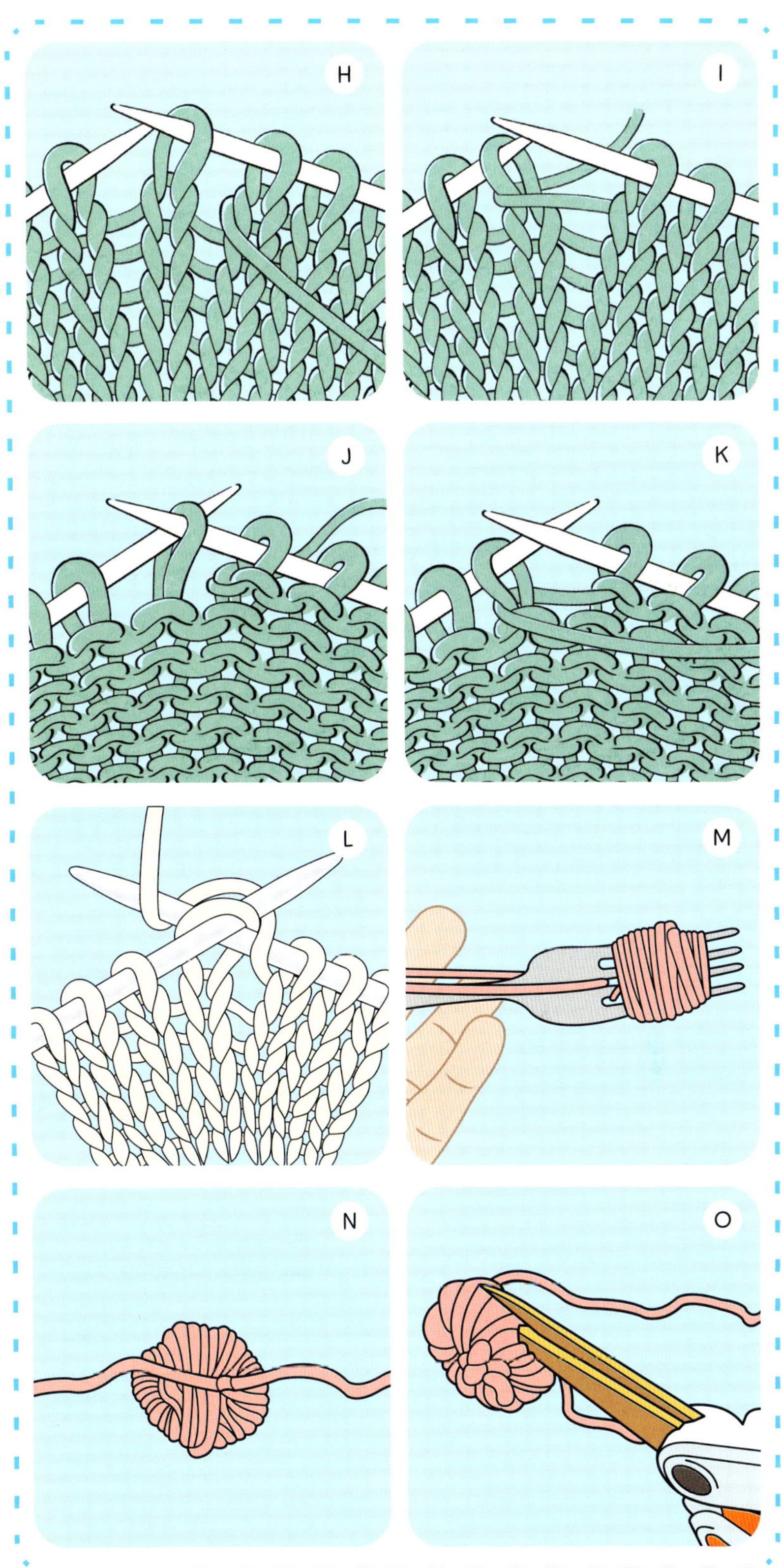

Increasing with kfb

This stitch will increase the stitch count by one. Knit the stitch but do not slip it off the left-hand needle. Insert the tip of the right-hand needle through the back of the same stitch **(A)** to knit it again in the back, then slip the worked stitch off the needle to make two stitches instead of one.

On a purl row, work in the same way but purling instead of knitting.

Decreasing with k2tog

This stitch will decrease the stitch count by one. Insert the tip of the right-hand needle through the next two stitches as if to knit **(B)**, and work them as if they were one stitch.

Decreasing with p2tog

To decrease on a purl row, insert the tip of the right-hand needle through the front of the next two stitches at the same time **(C)** and purl them as if they are one stitch.

Decreasing with ssk

This creates a left-slanting decrease. Slip the next two stitches from the left-hand needle to the right-hand needle knitwise without working them. Then insert the left-hand needle into the front of the two slipped stitches **(D)** and knit them together **(E)**.

Stranded colourwork

With this you will follow a chart to change colour, carrying the unused yarn until you need it again. When you get to the new colour on the chart, work the new yarn while holding the other yarn to the side. Twist the unused yarn with the working yarn every four stitches at the back of the work **(F shows K side, G shows P side)**. Try not to twist in the same place each row or you'll have a noticeable line in the knitted fabric, and keep the strands slightly loose.

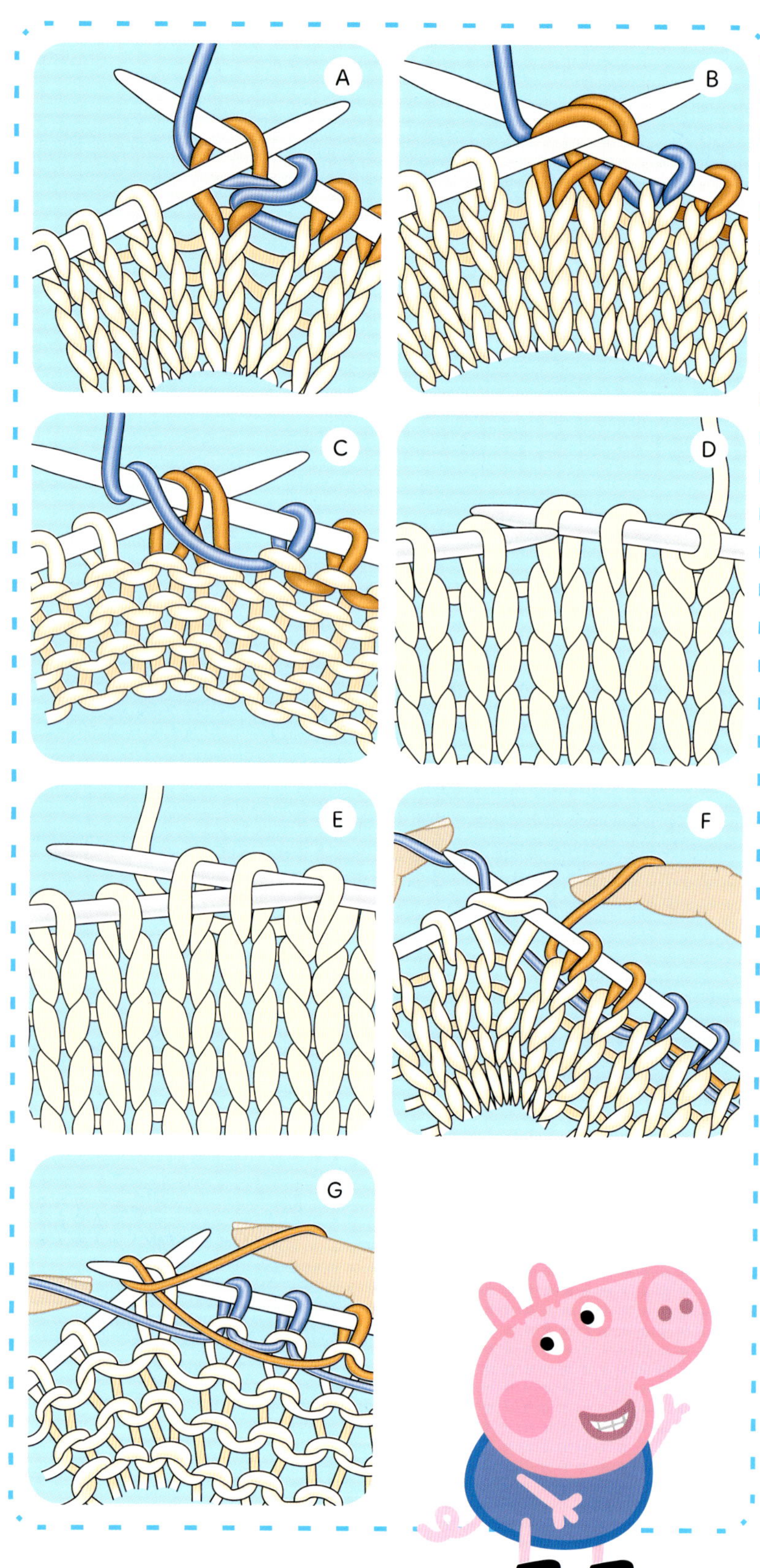

Sewing up

To join two pieces vertically with mattress stitch, place them side by side, right side up. Insert a tapestry needle under the horizontal bar between the first two stitches on the left and repeat on the right **(H)**. Work back and forth in this way to the end. Pull the yarn tight and watch the seam disappear! When joining pieces horizontally, insert the needle under the V point of the first stitch on one side and repeat on the other side **(I)**.

Straight stitch

A simple stitch that goes up and down through the fabric in a straight line. It's a great method to sew a small piece, such as a cheek or an eye, onto your knitted fabric or to sew details like a mouth or eyelashes **(J)**.

Chain stitch

Bring the thread through to the front, put the needle back at the same point then bring the tip out where the next stitch will start. Wrap the thread around the tip from left to right **(K)**, then pull the needle through and tighten the loop. Repeat to create a row of chains.

Satin stitch

A satin stitch is a great way to fill a small space, just sew straight stitches right next to each other **(L)**.

Duplicate stitch

Duplicate stitch (Swiss darning), adds colour to finished knitting. Bring your needle through the bottom point of a knit stitch, then insert it across the top of the knit stitch **(M)** and pull through. Return the needle to the bottom of the stitch to complete the duplicate stitch **(N)**. Repeat until the desired pattern has been achieved **(O)**.

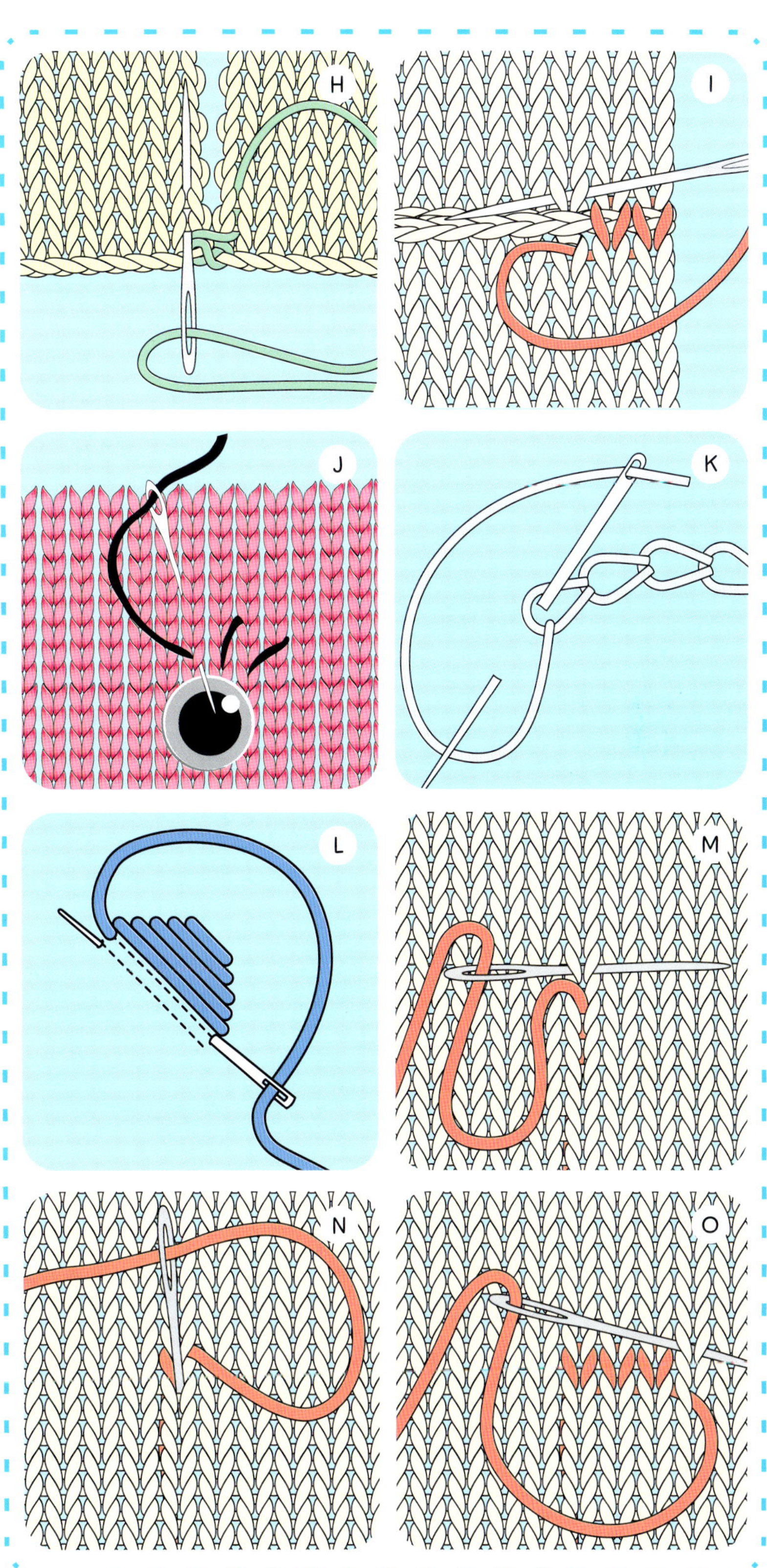

About the Author

Cilla Webb is an experienced knitter and designer with a passion for creating whimsical and charming knitted toys. She was born and raised in Belgium, where she was taught to knit at a young age by her mum. She soon became hooked on the craft. Now living in England, she started designing toys for her two boys who were always full of delightful suggestions for knitted toys. Since then, she has published three toy knitting books and has written numerous patterns for craft magazines. You can find more of Cilla's patterns on her website www.cillaspurls.co.uk. When not knitting, Cilla works as a Teacher of the Deaf in a resource base for deaf children.

Thanks

A big thank you to the team at David and Charles, especially Ame and Marie. This book would not have been possible without your support and encouragement.

Thank you to my friends and family for your ongoing support and enthusiasm and not judging me when I decided to take a suitcase full of yarn on our family holiday!

Above all, a big thank you to my two amazing boys who are quickly growing up to be even more amazing young men. You are my world.

Index

A DAVID AND CHARLES BOOK

David and Charles is an imprint of David and Charles, Ltd
Suite A, Tourism House, Pynes Hill, Exeter, EX2 5WS

First published in the UK and USA in 2025

A catalogue record for this book is available from the British Library.

ISBN-13: 9781446316535 paperback

This book has been printed on paper from approved suppliers and made from pulp from sustainable sources.

Printed in China by Asia Pacific Offset for:
David and Charles, Ltd
Suite A, Tourism House, Pynes Hill, Exeter, EX2 5WS

10 9 8 7 6 5 4 3 2 1

Publishing Director: Ame Verso
Publishing Manager: Jeni Chown
Project Editor: Marie Clayton
Tech Editor: Hannah Maltby
Lead Designer: Sam Staddon
Design: Dynamo Ltd
Pre-press Designer: Susan Reansbury
Illustrations: Kuo Kang Chen
Art Direction: Prudence Rogers
Photography: Jason Jenkins
Production Manager: Beverley Richardson

David and Charles publishes high-quality books on a wide range of subjects. For more information visit www.davidandcharles.com.

Share your makes with us on social media using #dandcbooks and follow us on Facebook and Instagram by searching for @dandcbooks.

Layout of the digital edition of this book may vary depending on reader hardware and display settings.